D1303009

100 CARS 100 YEARS

THE FIRST CENTURY OF THE AUTOMOBILE

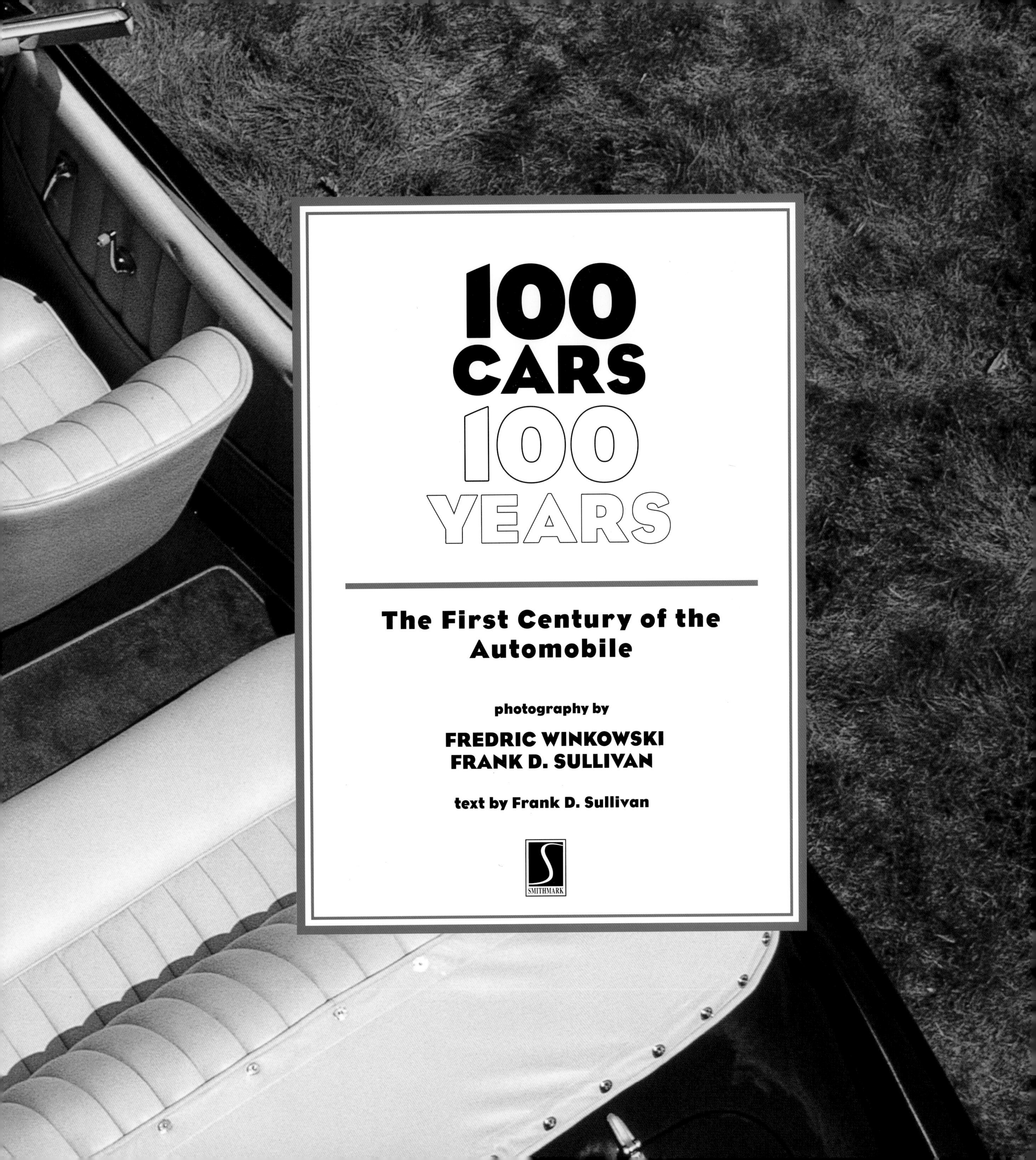

100 CARS 100 YEARS

The First Century of the Automobile

photography by

FREDRIC WINKOWSKI
FRANK D. SULLIVAN

text by Frank D. Sullivan

SMITHMARK

Copyright © 2000 by Fredric Winkowski and Frank D. Sullivan

All rights reserved. No part of this publication may be reproduced, stored in a retrieval system or transmitted in any form by any means electronic, mechanical, photocopying or otherwise without first obtaining written permission of the copyright owner.

This edition published in 2000 by SMITHMARK Publishers,
a division of U.S. Media Holdings, Inc.,
115 West 18th Street, New York, NY 10011.

SMITHMARK books are available for bulk purchase for sales promotion and premium use. For details write or call the manager of special sales, SMITHMARK Publishers, 115 West 18th Street, New York, NY 10011.

ISBN: 0-7651-1016-4

Printed in China

10 9 8 7 6 5 4 3 2 1

Library of Congress Cataloging-in-Publication Data

Winkowski, Fred.
100 cars 100 years : the first century of the automobile / photography by Fredric Winkowski, Frank D. Sullivan ; text by Frank D. Sullivan.
p. cm.
Includes index.
ISBN 0-7651-1016-4
1. Automobiles--History. I. Title: One hundred cars one hundred years. II. Sullivan, Frank, 1942–III. Title.

TL15.W56 1999
629.222'09--dc21 99-047737

C O N T E N T S

TERMOMETRO
ACQUA

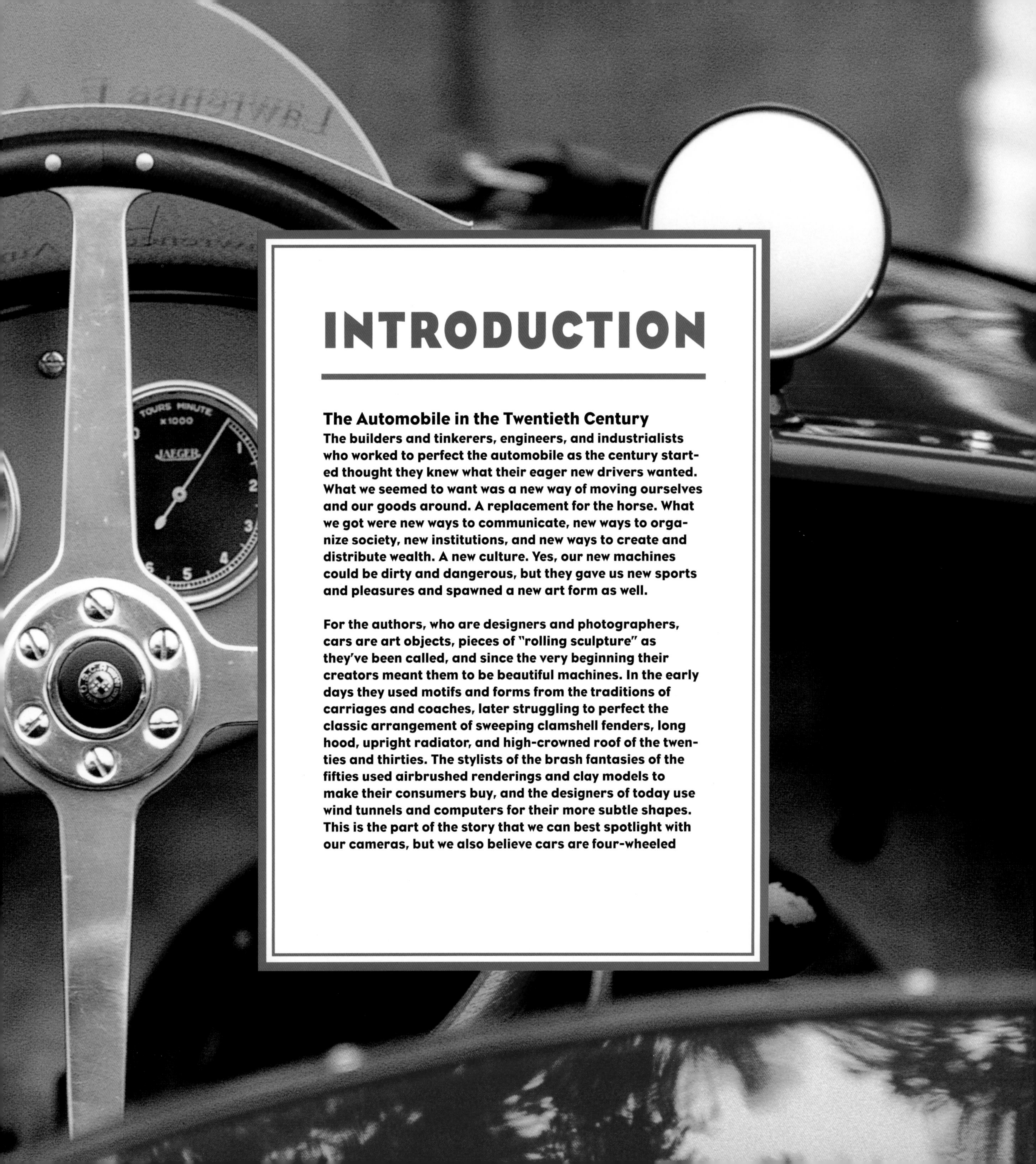

INTRODUCTION

The Automobile in the Twentieth Century

The builders and tinkerers, engineers, and industrialists who worked to perfect the automobile as the century started thought they knew what their eager new drivers wanted. What we seemed to want was a new way of moving ourselves and our goods around. A replacement for the horse. What we got were new ways to communicate, new ways to organize society, new institutions, and new ways to create and distribute wealth. A new culture. Yes, our new machines could be dirty and dangerous, but they gave us new sports and pleasures and spawned a new art form as well.

For the authors, who are designers and photographers, cars are art objects, pieces of "rolling sculpture" as they've been called, and since the very beginning their creators meant them to be beautiful machines. In the early days they used motifs and forms from the traditions of carriages and coaches, later struggling to perfect the classic arrangement of sweeping clamshell fenders, long hood, upright radiator, and high-crowned roof of the twenties and thirties. The stylists of the brash fantasies of the fifties used airbrushed renderings and clay models to make their consumers buy, and the designers of today use wind tunnels and computers for their more subtle shapes. This is the part of the story that we can best spotlight with our cameras, but we also believe cars are four-wheeled

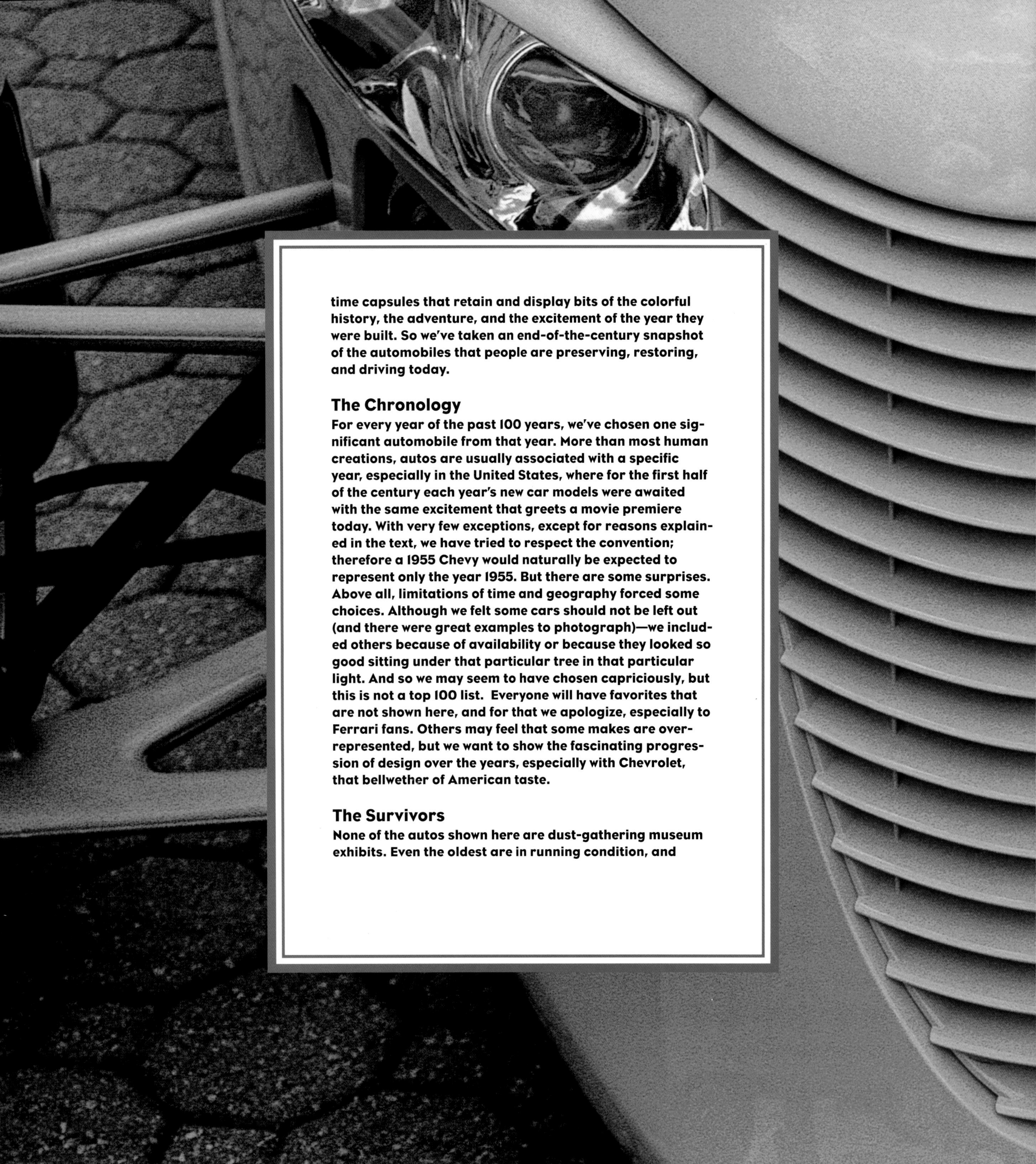

time capsules that retain and display bits of the colorful history, the adventure, and the excitement of the year they were built. So we've taken an end-of-the-century snapshot of the automobiles that people are preserving, restoring, and driving today.

The Chronology

For every year of the past 100 years, we've chosen one significant automobile from that year. More than most human creations, autos are usually associated with a specific year, especially in the United States, where for the first half of the century each year's new car models were awaited with the same excitement that greets a movie premiere today. With very few exceptions, except for reasons explained in the text, we have tried to respect the convention; therefore a 1955 Chevy would naturally be expected to represent only the year 1955. But there are some surprises. Above all, limitations of time and geography forced some choices. Although we felt some cars should not be left out (and there were great examples to photograph)—we included others because of availability or because they looked so good sitting under that particular tree in that particular light. And so we may seem to have chosen capriciously, but this is not a top 100 list. Everyone will have favorites that are not shown here, and for that we apologize, especially to Ferrari fans. Others may feel that some makes are over-represented, but we want to show the fascinating progression of design over the years, especially with Chevrolet, that bellwether of American taste.

The Survivors

None of the autos shown here are dust-gathering museum exhibits. Even the oldest are in running condition, and

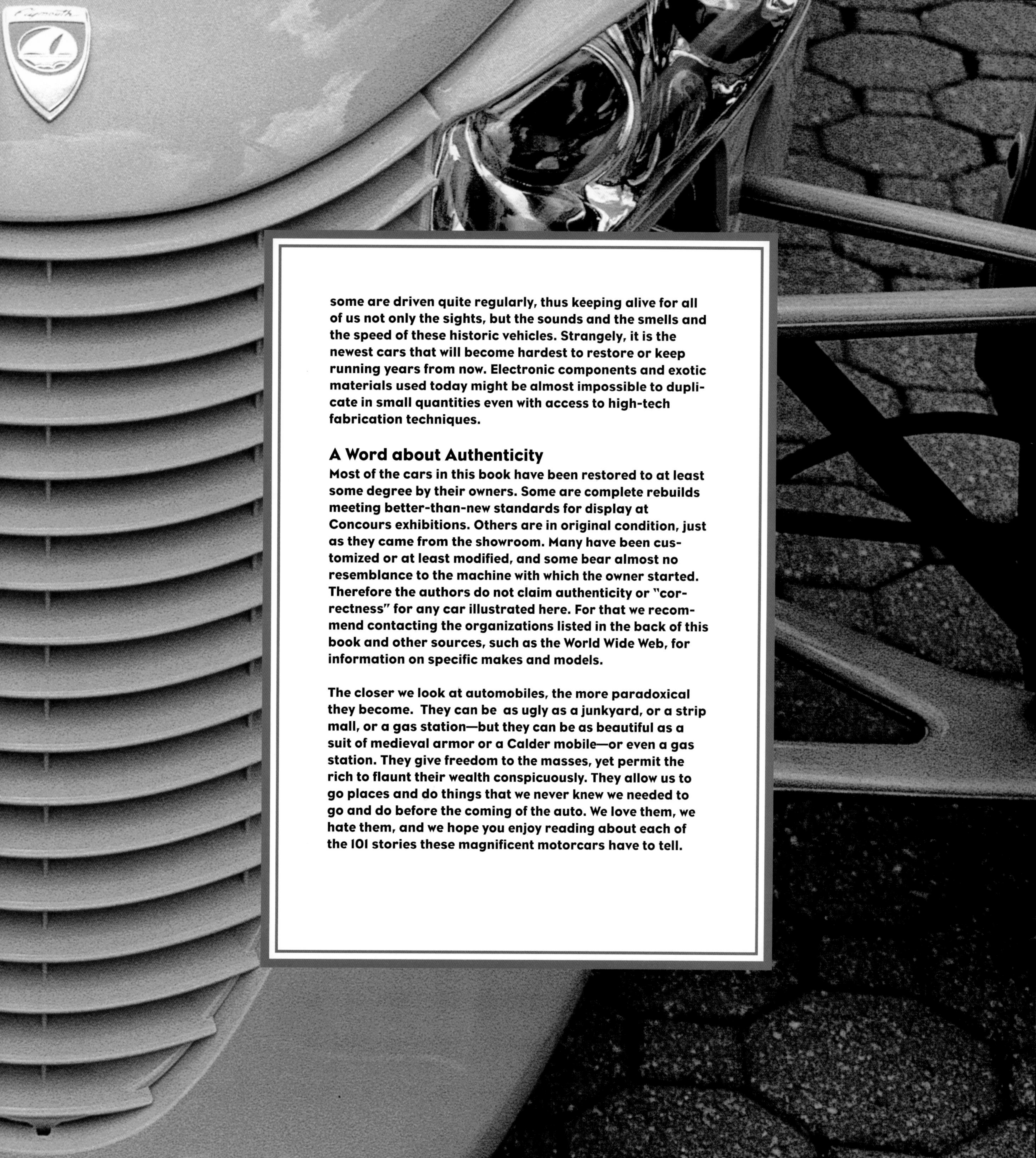

some are driven quite regularly, thus keeping alive for all of us not only the sights, but the sounds and the smells and the speed of these historic vehicles. Strangely, it is the newest cars that will become hardest to restore or keep running years from now. Electronic components and exotic materials used today might be almost impossible to duplicate in small quantities even with access to high-tech fabrication techniques.

A Word about Authenticity

Most of the cars in this book have been restored to at least some degree by their owners. Some are complete rebuilds meeting better-than-new standards for display at Concours exhibitions. Others are in original condition, just as they came from the showroom. Many have been customized or at least modified, and some bear almost no resemblance to the machine with which the owner started. Therefore the authors do not claim authenticity or "correctness" for any car illustrated here. For that we recommend contacting the organizations listed in the back of this book and other sources, such as the World Wide Web, for information on specific makes and models.

The closer we look at automobiles, the more paradoxical they become. They can be as ugly as a junkyard, or a strip mall, or a gas station—but they can be as beautiful as a suit of medieval armor or a Calder mobile—or even a gas station. They give freedom to the masses, yet permit the rich to flaunt their wealth conspicuously. They allow us to go places and do things that we never knew we needed to go and do before the coming of the auto. We love them, we hate them, and we hope you enjoy reading about each of the 101 stories these magnificent motorcars have to tell.

1900
Panhard et Levassor Rear Entrance Touring Car

We begin in Europe. As the century turned, thousands of autos traveled the roads of Germany, France, and Britain. The Continental view of the motorcar was as an emblem of wealth and status, or as a speedy and dangerous sporting machine. Rene Panhard and Emile Levassor started building their cars in 1891, and after Emile drove for a grueling 48 hours to victory in the 1895 Paris-Bordeaux-Paris race, Panhard moved to the forefront of European motoring.

At a time when American autos were really "horseless carriages," the 1900 Panhard was a proper motorcar, with a forward-mounted four-cylinder engine under a true hood and twin chains driving the rear wheels. After it appeared at the first New York auto show in Madison Square Garden in 1900, it was bought by a California Gold Rush millionaire for around $6000. A well-traveled car in its early years, it journeyed to Cuba, Brazil, and Argentina on its way around the Horn to California, then toured Japan in 1902 or 1903, by which time 1000 Panhards a year were being built.

1900-1909

Sputtering and wheezing and scaring the horses, the new century rolls in on gasoline-powered buggy wheels. First in Europe, then in America, one-cylinder carriages from Olds, Panhard, and Packard, quickly evolve into roaring racers, sumptuous conveyances, and even practical transport.

1901 Packard Model C Runabout

Not far from the Panhard at the 1900 New York auto show stood the new Model C Packard, a near duplicate of this stunning red runabout. This is the 103rd Packard built, and the sixth oldest remaining. The award-winning-car's wood body is original, as are the wire wheels and running lights. Colors are as in the original, and patent-leather fenders add some sparkle. It is an elegant and dependable machine. In 1989, its New Jersey owner completed the 58-mile London-to-Brighton run held each year for pre-1904 cars. But unlike the Panhard, the Packard is basically a motorized buggy. Its 10- or 12-hp, one-cylinder engine sits horizontally under the driver's seat and can push the car to 25 mph. With optional rear seats 5 feet above the ground, higher speeds would seem imprudent.

James Ward Packard's "buggy" boasted advanced features: a steering wheel, an H-gate shift pattern, and an automatic spark advance. Moneyed buyers, such as William Rockefeller and magnate William Joy, took notice. Mr. Joy also purchased an interest in the company, overseeing its move to Detroit in 1901. By 1904 the classic Packard radiator shape emerged, and great things lay ahead.

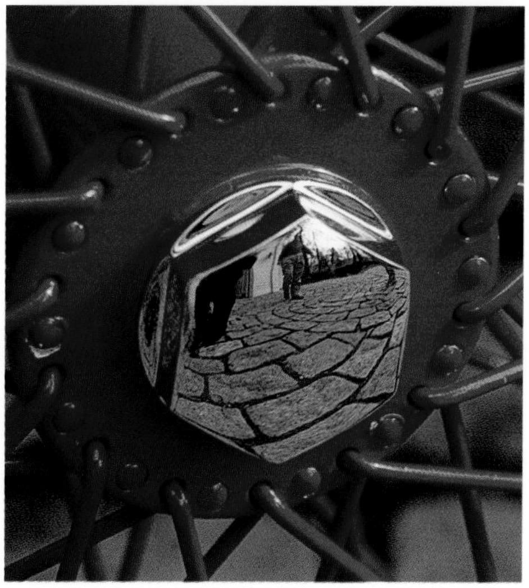

1902 Northern Runabout

It might just have been possible to drive this Northern Runabout across the country in 1902. In 1903, a Packard Model F made it from San Francisco to New York City in 61 days, but paved roads at this time were nonexistent, gasoline considered a dangerous explosive, and parts hard to come by. This particular machine, however, made the coast-to-coast trek in 1994! It is the oldest automobile ever to travel across the United States.

At the tiller of the little Northern was Raymond Carr, a successful real-estate developer with an adventurous spirit. His 2500-mile trek in the Northern put him in the "Guinness Book of World Records" and started a series of journeys in other antique cars that took him from Beijing to Paris and from Anchorage to Bangor.

The tiny 5-hp one-cylinder buggy was obviously "Built for Business," as its slogan claimed.

1903
Oldsmobile Curved-Dash Runabout

The curved-dash Olds is a "merry looking car," just as the song says. With its sleigh-like nose and light-footed stance, the car looks eager for an outing. Yet classical curves and Shaker-style functionality convey a simple dignity as well. This 1903 Model R, only minimally restored, shows off the optional buggy top, the windows of which are stored in the leather bag nestled behind the dash. Its rear-mounted engine, a bulky 4.5-inch-bore by 6-inch-stroke, one-cylinder type, cranks out about 5 hp.

This black-and-dark-red Olds still runs dependably today. Dependability and a bargain price of $650 made Ransom E. Olds' runabout a runaway best-seller, especially with the rising middle class, which craved the freedom waiting out beyond the city limits. Sales in 1901 were about 425; by 1903 about 4000 left the Lansing, Michigan, factory. By 1907 the petite curved dash was phased out as Oldsmobile misguidedly chased the luxury market. The company became part of General Motors in 1908, where it remains today—America's oldest automobile manufacturer.

1904
Cadillac Model B

In 1902, when ex-Ford backers decided to start an automobile company in Detroit with engine builder Henry Leland, they of course could not use the Ford name. Cadillac, the name they chose, was appropriate; a French explorer named Cadillac had put Detroit on the map, and so in its way did Leland's auto. The first model, introduced in 1903, and the slightly larger Model B illustrated, were unassuming in appearance, but beautifully crafted mechanically—a result of Henry Leland's career as a precision machinist. Parts were not machined to fit one car only, but were designed to be fully interchangeable, a first for automobiles. With its price of only $800 to $900, the public loved the new Cadillac. The first year's production sold out in a matter of weeks, while in 1904 production totaled 2300—more than any other American car.

Brookline Museum exhibits this sparkling red-and-white Model B with a surrey top. Rear entrance to the tonneau seats in back meant the car would be backed up to the curb so passengers could climb aboard.

1905 American Mercedes

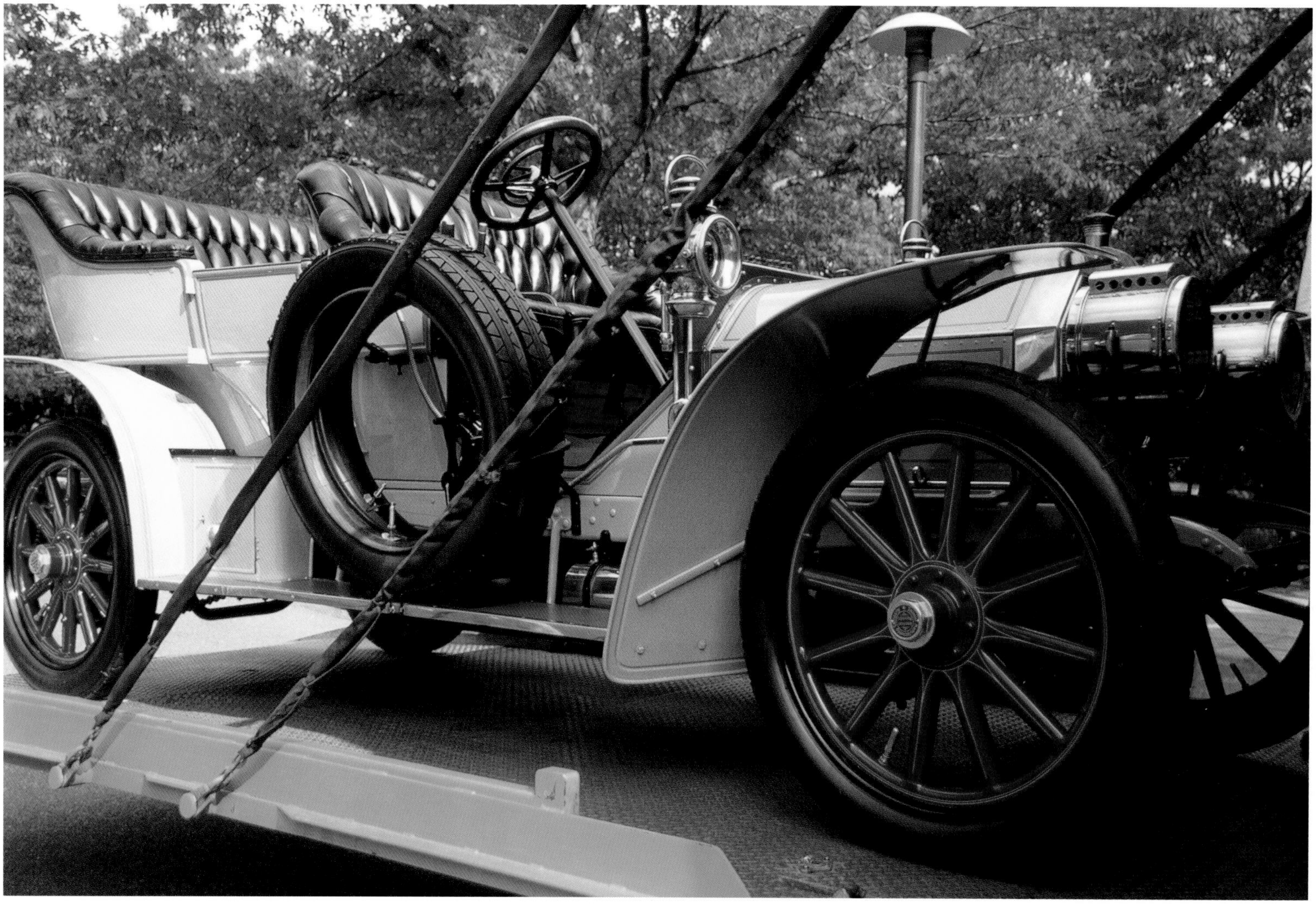

As early as 1888, Gottlieb Daimler had attempted to start assembly of Mercedes automobiles in the United States, encouraged by none other than piano merchant William Steinway. But it wasn't until 1904 that production started, in Steinway's New York piano factory. Mercedes were the first foreign cars to be built in America.

No one knows how many Mercedes autos were built here, but this 1905 Touring Car is almost certainly the only survivor. The precious machine seen here is being carefully loaded into its transporter after a rare appearance at the Lehigh Concours d'Elegance in Pennsylvania. A grandly scaled car on a 127-inch wheelbase, powered by a huge four-cylinder engine of almost 7 liters displacement, it drew immediate notice, and sales were brisk. Several of its features were borrowed by the more expensive American makes to impart that "Continental" quality to their deluxe models. Production might have continued indefinitely were it not for a ruinous fire that destroyed the factory in February 1907.

1906 Pope Hartford Model F

In the 1880s and 1890s, when bicycles were all the rage, Colonel Albert Pope built a bicycle empire. His "Bicycle Trust" comprised 45 firms. He resolved to do the same in the automotive world. Of the many Pope automobiles—among them, the Columbia, the Pope-Toledo, and the Pope-Tribune—the Pope-Hartford was the longest lived. Built in Pope's headquarters city of Hartford, Connecticut, the first Model B was a small single-cylinder car with a "coal scuttle" hood. By 1906, the Model F shown here had added 20 inches to its wheelbase and had become a four-cylinder touring car with a unique bell-shaped radiator.

Survivors such as this one, seen here not far from its birthplace at the Greenwich Connecticut Concours, bear out its reputation as a stolid, dependable car. After Colonel Pope's death in 1909, however, his empire disintegrated. Pope-Hartford went into receivership in 1913 and by 1914 was no more.

1907

1907
Renault 45 Racer

Louis Renault, along with his two older brothers, started building autos in a shed behind his parents' home in 1899, and 100 years later, the company has become one of the world's largest car manufacturers. From the beginning, the brothers Renault raced their cars; their greatest early victory being the first Grand Prix de France in 1906.

Wealthy American William K. Vanderbilt, Jr., was so impressed with the winning car that, it is said, he ordered half a dozen for his friends. The one shown here was owned by Harry Payne Whitney. Unmistakably a Renault, it has the "crocodile" hood and dash-mounted radiator that were trademarks of the breed until the late twenties. The four-cylinder engine, though only two-thirds the size of the 1906 racer's, still displaced 450 cubic inches and could push the car to 80 or 85 mph. A similar machine won the first 24-hour race held at Morris Park, New York, in September 1907.

1908
Stanley Steamer

To stretch a point a bit, the Stanley brothers, Francis and Freelan, might be seen as the Wright Brothers of the auto world. Their "Stanley Steamers" were certainly icons of the early Automobile Age. The rounded radia-torless hood hiding the boiler was the universally recognized mark of a Stanley until 1914.

They were quiet and clean, with power to spare. By 1906, more than 600 were being produced annually, and the slab-sided Stanley "Rocket" racer had torn up Ormond Beach, Florida, going more than 2 miles per minute. No airplane would beat that speed for more than six years. On the debit side, all Steamers were slow to warm up, and unless a recycling condenser was used, water stops had to be made every 50 to 100 miles. There were rumors of boil-er explosions. When gasoline-powered cars got self starters after 1912, losing their bothersome cranks, steam cars began a gradual slide to oblivion. Stanley sold its last Steamer in 1927.

This 1908 model F, seen scooting across Lehigh University's campus, is powered by a two-cylinder engine and sold originally for $1500.

Stanley

1909
Thomas Flyer 6-40

Around the World in 169 days! In July 1908, a Thomas Flyer—built in Buffalo, New York—chugged into Paris, beating five European competitors in a race west from New York overland across North America, Asia, and Europe. The winning car was basically a stock four-cylinder Flyer touring car. Thomas' publicists and sales force ballyhooed the Flyer as the World's toughest car. What went unreported were the preparations that had preceded the contest. E. R. Thomas was in financial trouble and saw the coming race as his company's salvation. Remaining cash was spent on spare parts to be strategically cached around the world—enough, it is rumored, to rebuild the car three times over. The gamble paid off—the Flyer won and sales soared, for a while. But as a bevy of new models appeared and prices jumped, Thomas grew complacent, quality control slipped, and like so many early winners, the Thomas Flyer faded into legend.

The striking red 1909 Thomas Flyer pictured here is not so different from the world-circling Flyer; it has a six-cylinder engine and a shaft rather than a chain drive.

THE · THOMAS · FLYER
T
E·R·THOMAS MOTOR CO.
BUFFALO. U.S.A.

1910
E-M-F Model 30

In 1910, the Model T Ford was gaining recognition as an incredible value by the driving public. The man who had helped to set up the production line for the Model T in 1908 was Walter Flanders, the "F" in E-M-F. Along with his partners Barney Everitt and William Metzger, he hoped to trump Ford with a larger, better-built car priced only slightly higher. The E-M-F was a quality product, as this handsome red machine, pictured on the lawn at the Brookline Museum of Transportation, shows. They were larger than the "T," with 30-hp motors, half-elliptic springs on all wheels, and a generally higher level of finish than Henry's "Tin Lizzie." Though they sold well, upwards of 15,000 in 1910, production of the Model T doubled and doubled again in succeeding years. Walter Flanders launched his own low-priced car, the Flanders 20, to go toe to toe with Ford. Studebaker took over the E-M-F plant, and by 1912, the name was gone.

1910-1919

Henry Ford gets his production line moving and that suits America to a "T." Other makers are forced to regroup and combine, eventually becoming the "Big Three" of today. The newborn auto empires seem hardly touched by the Great War. Instead they focus on selling to increasingly choosy American motorists.

1911

1911 Corbin Model 40 Roadster

Roadsters were excitement in the teen years of our century—gutsy sports cars with names like the Moon, the Mercer Raceabout, and the Stutz Bearcat, evocative names even today. Modeled after European road-racing machines, they were basically monster engines, with two bucket seats and a big gas tank mounted on a rugged frame.

This is the only known Corbin Model 40 roadster to survive. It is true to breed, with no windshield or doors, and precious little to hang onto at speed. Its owner, a New Hampshire man, restored the car more than 30 years ago and still loves to drive it flat out. The typically garish paint scheme dates from the late sixties as does the cylindrical gas tank, reportedly built from old iron lungs. Numerous medals and badges garnered by the Corbin roadster line its rudimentary trunk.

Connecticut-based Corbin dropped out of car manufacture in 1912 to return to its well-known hardware-and-lock business as American Hardware.

1912 Ford Model T Runabout

Henry Ford had been making the Model T now for four years, and he thought he just about had it right. There were 13,000 near-duplicates of this dark blue 1912 runabout sold along with more than 50,000 other Model T's, all for much less than $1000 apiece. People would joke about the "Flivver," but they pretty much agreed with Henry. Almost any American with a steady job could now own a car.

High wheels and a sturdy frame, with a simple, durable 20-hp, four-cylinder engine and good gas mileage added up to a formula that could and did last another 15 years. With just a little tweaking and a minor restyling job, the 1913 Model T's started coming down the world's first moving assem-

bly line. Production efficiency increased ten times over! Not only could Ford produce 300,000 cars the next year, but he could pay his workers a princely $5 a day and slash the price of his cars. A revolution was beginning.

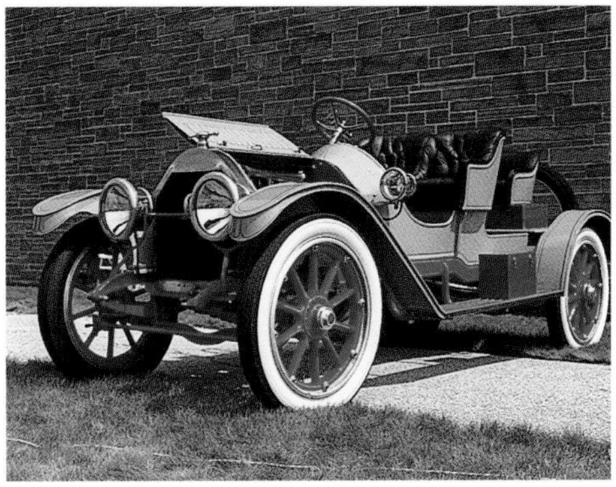

1913 Cadillac Roadster

What appears to be a beautifully restored 1913 Cadillac roadster is really a hybrid. After heroic work on what looked like a hopeless 1911 chassis and engine, the Pennsylvania owner decided he preferred the 1913 Cadillac bodies. They had been redesigned that year with a smoother cowl line and had inside-mounted controls. Therefore an almost totally rebuilt 1913 body has been grafted onto the frame after adjusting it to fit the 4-inch-shorter wheelbase. The front fenders, however, have the angular look of the 1911 models.

Under the hood sits a gleaming 30-hp Cadillac four with individually copper-jacketed cylinders. Even though nickel-plated brightwork was available for the 1913 models, this car looks resplendent in brass and deserving of the Cadillac motto, "Standard of the World," first used that year.

1914 Stearns-Knight

F. M. Stearns built motorcars for affluent solid citizens with a sporting bent. The white-edged radiator, patented in 1909, appeared on well-built, costly, but never flamboyant, cars until the crash of 1929 killed off the marque.

By 1914 the buying public wanted more than just a reliable, quality automobile. For the $5000 that this six-cylinder Knight-engined touring car would cost when new, discerning drivers wanted some style. The new bodies Stearns introduced that year typified the continuing trend away from the look of the horse-drawn carriage. Most notable is the sweeping line from radiator cap to rear seat. Other touches emphasize that horizontal look and help the parts of the car begin to meld into a unit, from the curve of the front fender into the running board to the discreetly enclosed frame skirting. Even the cumbersome top of the Stearns juts aggressively forward. With these timid steps began the quest for long, low, road-hugging machines that continues today.

1915
Brewster Transformable Town Car

With a coachbuilding tradition dating back to 1810, the Brewster firm approached automobile design in a conservative, almost reactionary, way. For ten years, starting in 1915, this venerable company built its own motorcars, after supplying bodies to other automakers since the turn of the century. Almost all were larger, expensive machines using the finest materials and borrowing themes from Brewster's hundred-plus years of carriage design to evoke for wealthy buyers the aura of the Gilded Age.

Typifying Brewster at its sumptuous best is the 1915 Transformable Town Car seen at the Greenwich Concours. The unusual body design resembles a closed landau, but the top and front divider fold down to convert to a totally open car. The typical oval radiator of the Brewster graces a simple body shell, extravagantly finished in stripes of burgundy and cream and sporting a wicker trunk, surely *de rigueur* for picnics.

1916
Dodge Model 30 Touring Car

The Dodge Brothers made their break with Ford in 1914. After supplying Henry for years with engines and other parts, they introduced their own auto as the year ended. It was America's first production car with an all-welded-steel body. The durable body and dependable 35-hp L-head engine of the Dodge made it the perfect scout car for General Pershing's 1916 pursuit of insurgent leader Pancho Villa's rebels across the badlands of Mexico.

The war raging across Europe seemed not to affect sales of the new Dodge. By the end of 1916, Dodge Brothers ranked fourth in the industry, but war fever spread among Americans until the United States entered the Great War on the Allied side in April 1917. This 1917 Dodge Tourer, recognizable by headlights mounted a bit farther forward than on earlier models, sports a patriotic display typical of the World War I years. As Pershing's adventure proved, the cars were rugged enough for combat duty. Many thousands of Dodges, including their newly introduced trucks, made their way into the military and service "Over There."

1917
GMC Model 16AA Ambulance

Sadly, too many of the doughboys going overseas to "Hang the Kaiser from a Sour Apple Tree" made part of their return journey in an ambulance like this one. By the end of 1917, General Motors was producing 50 Model 16AA military ambulances daily. Developed from the pre-war four-cylinder Model 16 with shaft drive, the GMC served alongside Ford Model T ambulances like that driven by Ernest Hemingway. They had their work cut out for them; over 200,000 Americans were wounded before fighting ended in November 1918.

Joseph Janichko of Pennsylvania built the GMC seen here from an assemblage of parts he bought from the Aberdeen proving grounds in Maryland. Almost everything was there, including cold-weather radiator shutters and most of the running lights. The front fenders are cobbled up, however, being flat, not curved, as in the original. New wood and canvas, plus a set of uniforms, stretchers, and other medical equipment, capped off by a rare gas-attack siren complete the re-creation.

1918 Straker-Squire X2

What better way to draw attention to your new racing car than to "dazzle paint" it? The driver, Bertie Kensington-Moir, had done a stint in the British Royal Navy, whose ships were painted in wide, angular swaths of black and white to confuse German submariners.

The prototype cars first ran right after the Armistice in November 1918, and first races began in 1920. The black-and-white "camouflage" finish and elongated radiator cowl were 1921 additions. Under that camouflage was a capable machine with a six-cylinder, 3.9-liter, overhead-cam engine and aluminum pistons that eventually gave 115 hp. The X-2 lapped Britain's famous Brooklands track, where this example is preserved today, at over 100 mph. Racing success had come to other Straker-Squire cars since the marque's debut in 1906, most notably R. S. Witchell's "PDQ" of 1911 to 1912. Sydney Straker had planned to market a passenger car but settled for sales of close to sixty 3.9-liter racers and tourers based on the doughty X2.

1919 Ford Model T Speedster

Imagine yourself a well-heeled college student in the mid-1920s, enamored of racy autos like the Mercer and Stutz, but driving your dad's hand-me-down, old Model T. If you wanted speed or the appearance of speed, you'd get yourself down to the local "Gasoline Alley." Now that Fords were selling in the millions, there were hundreds of what would come to be called "aftermarket" suppliers selling parts to soup up your car—anything from engine accessories to whole new bodies, such as that fitted to this bold yellow speedster seen at the Rhinebeck Aerodrome in Rhinebeck, New York. Though the fenders are vintage 1911 or 1912, the body, by Champion, dates from around 1919. With peaked radiator, leather-strapped hood with "streamlined" louvers, bucket seats, and cylindrical gas tank, you had an instant sports car. Paint a few rah-rah school slogans on your jalopy, and you were ready for the Homecoming game. Twenty-three skiddoo!

Ford

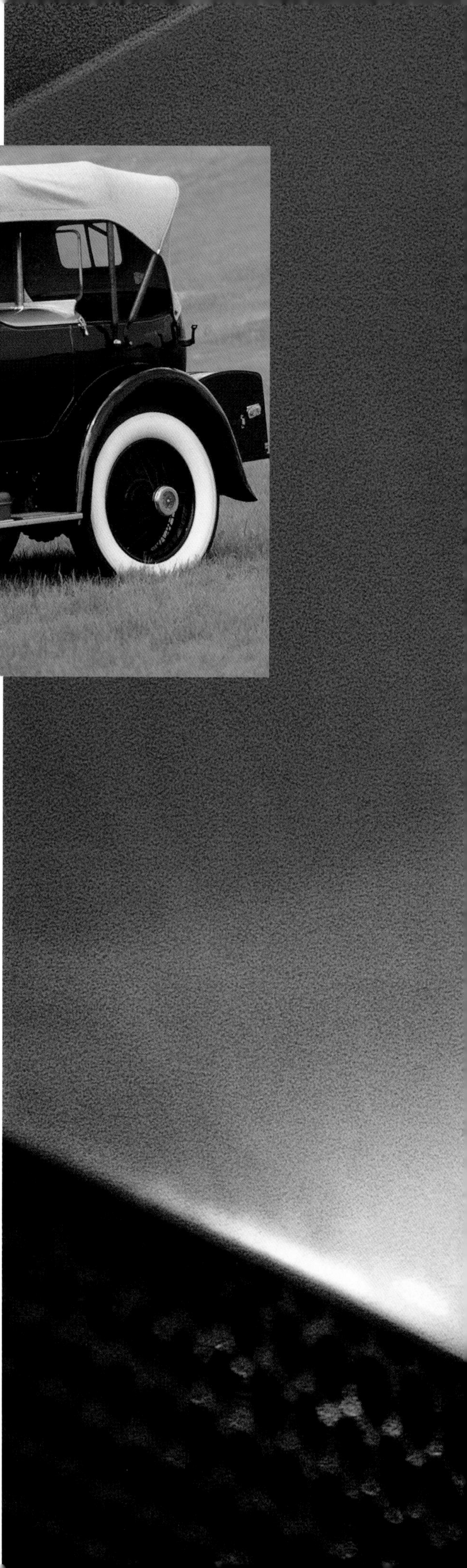

1920 Rolls-Royce Silver Ghost Dual-Cowl Tourer

It is "The Best Car in the World," and though that slogan can be challenged today by many marques, for most of the century Charles Rolls and Frederick Royce's machines had fair claim to the title. Royce, though working class in origin, picked up engineering and business skills enough to build a creditable car, concentrating on durability and reliability. Rolls, a well-born young engineer and racing driver, who had recently started selling luxury motorcars, tested one of Royce's new autos in 1903. He found it to be the best available, and when the two got together in 1904, they brought their emphasis on quality to heights of near obsession. Rolls-Royce engines and chassis components, sans bodies, were machined, built, and tested to state-of-the-art tolerances, then road-tested and completely disassembled, rebalanced, and rebuilt, and then road-tested once again after the bespoke bodies were mounted.

This particular Silver Ghost, the model built from 1907 to 1925, is handsome yet seemingly unprepossessing. It was ordered before World War I as a sensible closed sedan before wartime exigencies forced Rolls-Royce to the production of aero engines and military vehicles. Not until 1920 was the auto delivered. By then the customer's interests had changed, so within a year a sportier, open touring body by Windover was fitted, highlighted by a buffed aluminum hood. It spent most of its life in southern France.

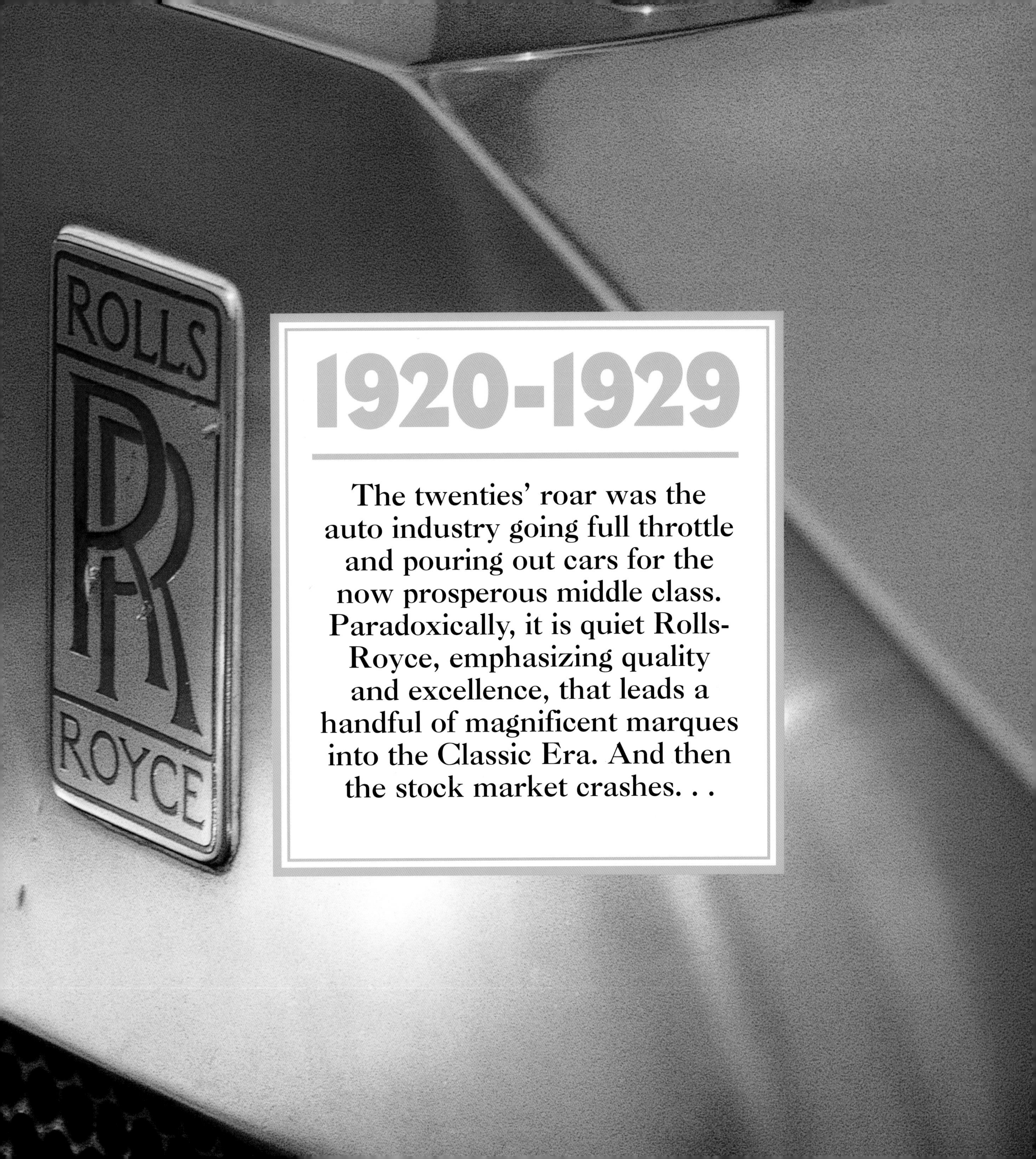

1920-1929

The twenties' roar was the auto industry going full throttle and pouring out cars for the now prosperous middle class. Paradoxically, it is quiet Rolls-Royce, emphasizing quality and excellence, that leads a handful of magnificent marques into the Classic Era. And then the stock market crashes. . .

1921
H.C.S. Series II Roadster

Harry C. Stutz was bought out when the company he founded, maker of the renowned Stutz Bearcat, went public. Remaining in Indianapolis, Indiana, he jumped right back into the car-making business. The new auto used Stutz's initials, H.C.S, and traded upon his celebrity and good name with ads using the slogan: "The Car Born with a Reputation." The first examples sold quickly, starting in 1920.

They were quality cars, comparable to the smaller Stutzes, using the same 120-inch wheelbase and a similar 50-hp, four-cylinder engine (from Weidely instead of Wisconsin Motors). The difference was they sold for about $1000 less than a Stutz. Harry Stutz liked racy vehicles, so touches like the rakishly tilted windshield and the buckboard steps instead of running boards all reinforced the sporting image. A win at the Indianapolis 500 in 1923 by the "H.C.S. Special" only added to the performance aura surrounding the car. But, by 1924, an ill-conceived venture into taxicab production put a stop to the brief career of the H.C.S.

1922
Springfield Rolls-Royce

An American Rolls-Royce? Most assuredly, what with the pent-up demand for the legendary British auto in the United States after World War I and high import-tax surcharges. In 1921, Rolls started manufacture of their standard Silver Ghost model in Springfield, Massachusetts, the car being similar to the 1920 model shown previously, which was of course almost unchanged from the 1907 original. And, not to worry, the American Rolls would be crafted by "British mechanics under British supervision." By 1922, when this baby-blue Picadilly Roadster, once owned by the DuPonts was built, about 230 machines came off the line, most with custom-built bodies.

The time-honored six-cylinder engine was used on the long, 143.5-inch-wheelbase Silver Ghost until 1926, when the new Phantom replaced it both here and in England. Also at that time, the esteemed Brewster firm of coachbuilders was acquired by Rolls, ceasing production of their car to become suppliers of custom bodies for Rolls-Royce.

1923

1923 Hispano-Suiza H-6B

Atop the hood of every Hispano-Suiza is the graceful chrome sculpture of a flying stork designed by Bazin. Proud emblem of Hispano's World War I contribution to the allied victory, the stork—La Cigogne—had adorned the sides of SPAD fighter planes of the Third Escadrille, flown by French aces such as Georges Guynemer. All of these SPADs had been powered by Hispano-Suiza engines.

The Spanish-Swiss automaker's prewar Alfonso model proved popular, but the six-cylinder engine produced

by Swiss engineer Marc Birkigt made the Hispano-Suiza a world-class car. The H-6 model of 1919 could be fitted with custom formal limousine bodies or stripped down for flat-out racing with equal aplomb. French Aperitif magnate Andre Dubonnet flew SPADs during the war so he naturally chose the new H-6B as his racing mount. Dubonnet favored wooden construction, as seen in this 1923 H-6B dual-cowl skiff by Labourdette of Paris. Thousands of copper rivets hold thin strips of tulipwood to the body's ribs or formers, making for a light but strong hull like that of a speedboat or airplane.

1924 Voisin C-3 Salamanca

The brothers Voisin were among France's true aviation pioneers, flying first in 1907 and establishing the world's first aircraft production line soon after. In the Great War, Avions Voisin churned out thousands of stolid, conservative biplanes that, though obsolescent and slow, nevertheless formed the backbone of the French Air Force's bombing and observation forces. At the war's end, the bottom fell out of the military airplane market, and Gabriel, the surviving brother, turned to making automobiles.

What autos they were! Unlike Voisin's planes, his cars were daring and innovative. Case in point is this 1924 Model C-3 Salamanca (similar to the disappearing-top Brewster shown earlier) with body by Rothschild et Fils. From the towering foot-high Art Deco radiator mascot atop its nickel-and-German-silver radiator grille to its twin disk-wheeled spares, this machine exudes class. Aluminum body panels enclose a Knight-licensed sleeve-valve engine and a passenger compartment trimmed in brass and mahogany. Voisin seemed to resent potential customers who had the effrontery to consider being allowed to buy one of his creations. But the glitterati of the day lined up for them. Maurice Chevalier and H. G. Wells owned Voisins, and screen idol Rudolph Valentino had at least two.

1925
Bugatti Type 35

Ettore Bugatti trained as an artist; his father and brother also were sculptors and designers. Though he was a mechanical genius, his cars were works of art, and that is how we should look at them. The Type 35 is a Grand Prix racing machine, purely functional, yet its lines, curves, and masses are arranged with no less care than the later Bugatti Royale formal limousines. At the time of the Type 35's debut in 1924, Architect Le Corbusier's book *Towards a New Architecture* was causing an uproar, partly because automobile design was championed as a function-based discipline that architecture should emulate.

Ettore, however, had other concerns. His 2-liter, single-overhead-cam Type 35's were being regularly beaten in the 1925 season, so the Type 35B of 1926 had a larger engine and a supercharger. Racing number "8," a 1928 Type 35 TC (Targa Compressor) owned by Don Koleman of Massachusetts, shows off the larger cast-aluminum wheels with integral brake drums needed to handle the power of the supercharged 140-hp, 2.3-liter engine. A four-seat touring version of the 35B, called the Type 43, offered 112-mph speeds to the sporting set.

1926
AC Royal Roadster

This petite two-seater is a direct ancestor of the fire-breathing AC Cobras of the 1960s. The 1926 model Royal could be had, as shown here, with a four-cylinder Anzani engine of 1.5 liters or with a 2-liter, six-cylinder engine. It was this overhead-cam motor, which was very advanced for the time, that powered succeeding generations of AC cars until 1963. By then, the power plant, rated at 35 hp in the early twenties was pumping out 105 hp.

An AC machine similar to the one here was the first British car to win the Monte Carlo rally in 1926. The narrow-stanced Royal evolved in the thirties under new ownership into the first AC Ace, a timeless British sports car in the classic mold. It was the postwar Ace, designed by John Tojeiro and produced from 1953, that inspired American racer Carrol Shelby in 1963 to stuff a 428-cubic-inch Ford engine under its hood (plenty of room!) and produce the immortal Cobra.

7

1927
Bentley 3-Liter

Winner of the 24-hour Le Mans race in France this year was a Bentley very like this one. This was "Old Number 7," a 3-liter racer driven by Benjafield and Davis, who managed to spur the mangled car to victory after a crash at the infamous Whitehouse Corner involving all three of the Bentleys competing in the race. Thus began a streak of four Le Mans wins that stood unbeaten until the 1980s.

This particular 3-liter "Red Label" Speed Model, an eye-catching beast, though not quite in Concours condition, has led an eventful life. Originally possessing more sedate Vanden Plas coachwork, around 1947, the current body was fitted. The nonstandard "tall-style" radiator was well suited to the warm climate of Uganda, its home for many years.

Racing success was not enough to prevent Bentley's demise in the Depression, with takeover by Rolls-Royce in 1931. From then on, Bentley gradually seemed to become just a Rolls with new grillework, but lately such gems as the Bentley Turbo R have caught an echo of the glory days of 1927.

1928
Stutz Model BB Speedster

The Stutz car was born racing and died racing. A Stutz Blackhawk speedster took second place at Le Mans in 1928, nearly ending Bentley's four-year winning streak before it had fairly begun. At the first Indianapolis 500 in 1911, the new Stutz was "the car that made good in a day." When the production two-seat roadster pounced onto U.S. highways in 1912, its name became synonymous with guts and speed. This was the legendary Stutz Bearcat.

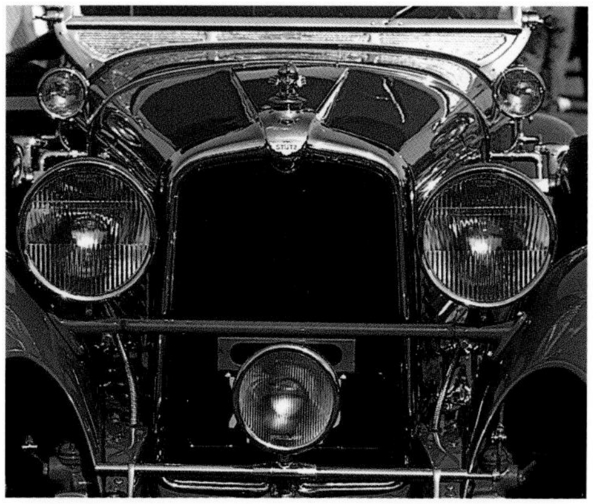

By the time this 1928 model BB four-seater premiered, Harry C. Stutz was long gone, and "Safety Stutz" was the slogan for cars that had become long, low, and stylish. Emulating a European model, however, it was known to have reserves of power and roadworthiness. The Continental theme continued in the very names of its models: Chantilly, Chamonix, Versailles. Ironically, Stutz failed because it could not keep up in the Depression-era horsepower race. A magnificent twin-overhead-cam-engine V-8 could not match the V-12 and V-16 engines from Lincoln and Cadillac. The company produced only six cars in 1934, though a Stutz won the Pike's Peak Climb that year.

1929
L-29 Cord Convertible Sedan

As the infant discipline of automobile design emerged in the late twenties, it was the L-29 Cord that showed the way. It may have seemed an engineering gimmick to put a car's drive wheels up front in 1929 (it is almost *de rigueur* today), but stylists and coachbuilders loved the car. With no driveshaft to perch the seats upon, cars could be long and low, and with a transmission in front, the radiator could be moved back behind the front wheels. Al Leamy, the young chief stylist for Cord, accented this feature with his raked and V-shaped radiator grille, one of the first on an American auto, that nestled snugly over the curving transmission cover. Other designers, notably Sakhnoffsky and the firm of LeBaron, produced award-winning designs for the Cord.

The L-29 shown here is a 1930 model, a convertible sedan unremarkable except for striking colors of cream and green, but long and low enough to make other cars around it seem gawky by comparison. Its transmission, whispering from between the front wheels, has a sound like no other. Unfortunately, the L-29 was discontinued in 1932; rumors persisted of mechanical problems and handling difficulties, but 5000 had been produced. When the Cord returned in 1936, it was a different breed, as we shall see.

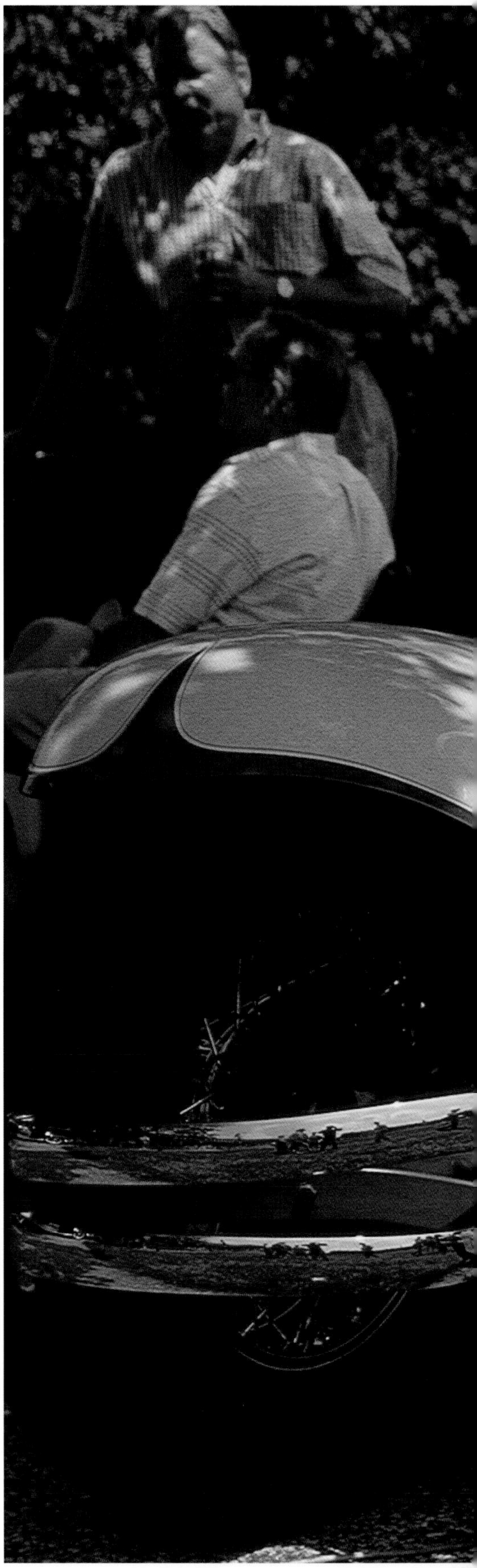

1998
Concours d'Elegance
of the Eastern United States
1998
1930
CORD
VICTOR PLUMBO
zymöl

1930 Packard Deluxe Eight Phaeton

Depression? What Depression? Maybe the original Newark, New Jersey, buyer of this Packard got out of the Market before the October 1929 crash. In any case, he was feeling flush. Though a custom-bodied car by coachbuilders like Rollston or Dietrich was out of the question, Packard had just the thing. For about $1300 more than the $3200 asked for the standard Custom Eight, Packard's own craftsmen would customize your car. Five inches would be added to the frame, colors and appointments would be your choice, and a host of options would be added to round out the Packard's already impressive list of amenities.

The Phaeton is the most desirable of classics; this model 745 sports an added adjustable tonneau windshield. Dual side-mounted spares were standard, as were painted disk wheels, but the bumper-mounted lights that swung with the car's steering were marvelous options. So were the spotlights, the chrome radiator stone shield, and the special "sliding boy" hood mascot. All this, in addition to Packard's straight-eight engine, new four-speed transmission, and shatterproof glass—the perfect car to reassure one's creditors.

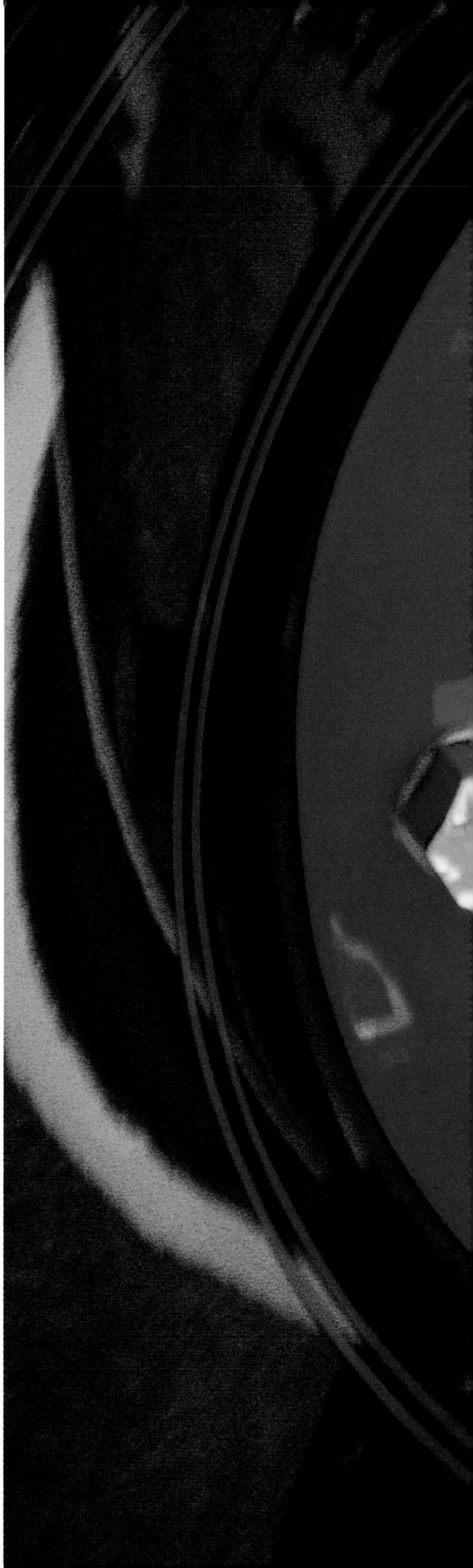

1930-1939

Worldwide Depression cannot kill a last flowering of the classic auto. Rich buyers of these Auburns, Imperials, and Duesenbergs seem unperturbed by bread lines and dust bowls. Those less well off are distracted from their cares by the streamlined future portrayed in the 1939 World's Fair.

1931
Auburn Model 8-98A Cabriolet

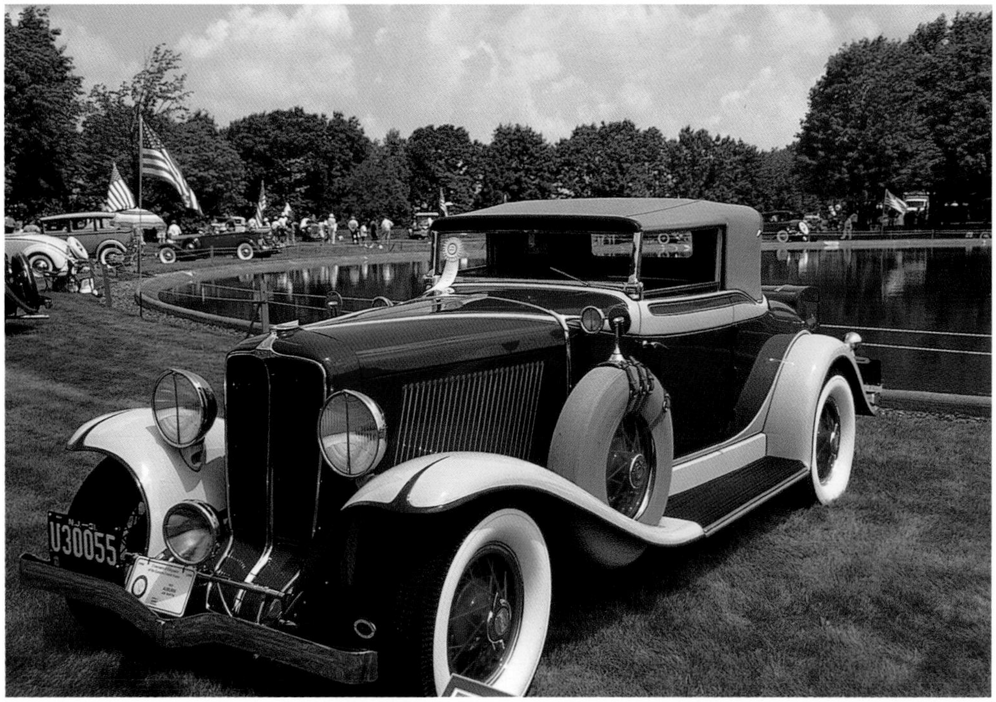

In 1924, a young sales phenomenon named E. L. Cord stormed in from the West Coast to revive the slumping Auburn Company. Using simple cosmetic styling ploys and a Lycoming straight-eight to replace the car's anemic six, he changed Auburn from a sleepy look-alike into a hot selling machine, doubling sales for three straight years.

By 1931, Mr. Cord's auto empire was expanding, and it seemed he could do no wrong. Auburn chief designer Al Leamy's L-29 Cord and Duesenberg Model J were still turning heads, and now it was Auburn's turn. The new 8-98 bodies were not radical, but Leamy's linear, flowing style and his use of color, evident in this maroon-and-blue-gray cabriolet, made the Auburn a standout. For its price of $1250, the combination of high style and 287-cubic-inch Lycoming could not be beat. Here was a classic for the masses. *Fortune* magazine said it was "the biggest package in the world for the price," and even as the Depression deepened, more than 28,000 were sold.

1932
Bugatti Type 55

Representing a true mixture of the racing and touring machine, this Bugatti shows, more than most Type 55's, how it was related to the highly successful Type 51 Grand Prix cars. As the Type 35 racer begat the sports model 43, so was the new racer's dual-overhead-camshaft engine used in slightly de-tuned form to produce a two-seat sports car designated the Type 55. Weighing less than 2200 pounds, the 135-hp car could be pushed to 115 mph, and levels of comfort were much improved over the pure racing machines.

The body was by Ettore's son Jean Bugatti, whose curvilinear style was less austere and rigorous than "Il Patron's" work. But the characteristic flowing lines of the typical Type 55's fenders are missing here, replaced by racing-cycle-type fenders. This lends credence to the belief that this car was originally intended as a Le Mans racer, at which time it would have been fitted with a four-passenger Wain and Fabric body.

1933

1933 Chrysler Imperial Convertible Sedan

High atop the Chrysler Building in Manhattan, there once was a futuristic showroom displaying the latest Chrysler motorcars. Chrysler's Art Deco monument had opened as the Depression began, expressing the company's growing awareness of good design as a selling tool. For a while in the early thirties, they were very good products indeed, as this prize-winning

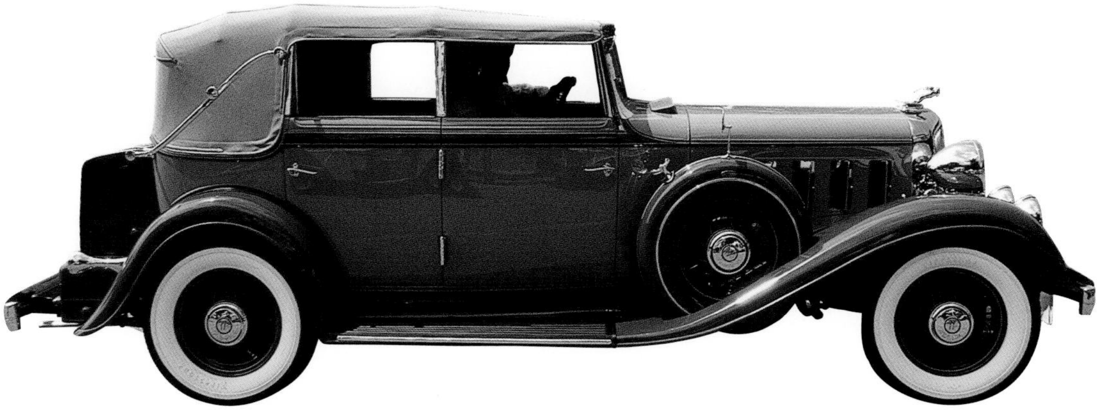

1933 Chrysler Imperial CQ demonstrates. When the 1932 models arrived, no secret was made of their borrowing much from the L-29 Cord and the Duesenberg. Their slanted V-grilled radiators, wind-split windshields, and lowered bodies spoke of Cord, while the "bow-tie" bumpers and chrome-trimmed rear fenders echoed the Duesy. For 1933, fenders sloped down in front to meet simplified bumpers. Twin trumpet horns and the leaping-gazelle mascot made for a striking front view. Of course engineering niceties such as high-compression engines and hydraulic brakes kept pace.

But the very next year, one of history's greatest styling fiascoes came to market: the still controversial Chrysler Airflow. Yes, they were aerodynamic, but they were engineered, not styled. The public hated them, and Chrysler shunned innovative body design until Virgil Exner's mid-fifties "Forward Look."

1934

1934 Packard Model 1107 Sport Phaeton

Here is Packard, one of the premier American automobiles at the top of its form. There are twelve cylinders under that unmistakable scalloped hood line fronted by an unshakably vertical V-shaped prow. A concession to streamlining shows in the delicately skirted front fenders. And which of today's cars could carry off a paint scheme like this with such nonchalance? Though there were more expensive American cars, none had the instant recognition, the understated cachet, of the Packard. Born with the century, Packard had always cultivated the carriage trade, keeping styling changes to a minimum, and quietly staying at the forefront of mechanical innovation. But the Depression sent sales spiraling downward.

Possibly modern marketing and branding practices could have solved Packard's dilemma, but in the end only Cadillac, Lincoln, and Imperial survived, and that was because of the cushion provided by their huge parent corporations

1935 Lincoln LeBaron Roadster

Since its inception in 1920, the Lincoln had been a ponderous, stodgy car. Lincolns were built with precision and were worth every dime of their high price, but that they were President Coolidge's favorite car speaks volumes about their style. This continued under Henry Ford, as he cared little for styling frills—"any color as long as it is black." As Henry's son Edsel made his presence known, this began to change. Edsel was an educated man with a love of the arts. In 1935 he set up a small styling studio with Bob Gregorie at its head. Gregorie, ex-naval architect and veteran of GM's "art and colour section," worked closely with Edsel until

the latter's death in 1943, producing all of Ford's cars up until the famous "bathtub" 1949 Mercury.

This 1935 Model K series 542 V-12 marks an intermediate step toward design landmarks such as the Zephyr and the Continental. The custom body firm of LeBaron placed a two-door coupe with rumble seat upon the 136-inch-wheelbase Lincoln, leading to an extremely long rear deck. Minimal use of chrome and dark finish on the very rounded hood and fenders used that year are suggestive of Ford hot-rods of the forties and fifties.

Elegance
United States
1998
1935
AUBURN
BRUCE EARLIN

1936
Auburn, Cord, Duesenberg

Auburn, Cord, Duesenberg—a holy trinity of American classic carmaking. And at its head, Errett Lobban Cord. The ambitious industrialist's empire-building continued while his auto holdings suffered; the three marques which seemed to offer so much would not survive another year.

Auburn updated its brand of low price combined with dramatic upscale styling and high performance in 1935. Two of the ultimate Auburns are shown here: a tan 1935 model 851 supercharged boattail speedster, and a red model 852 from 1936. They both wear the chromed exhaust pipes that engine to the ultimate luxury automobile and watch the sparks fly! This machine was the model "J," produced after Cord acquired Duesenberg in 1929, and available as bare chassis and engine only. Radiator grille and fenders were part of the package—as of course were those exhaust pipes. Even some cars without the supercharger, such as the red LeBaron Phaeton here, were ordered with the four chrome exterior exhausts. Coachbuilders outdid themselves with custom bodies for the Duesy, while the famous (and infamous) bid outrageous amounts for them. Less than 500 were crafted over a span of seven years.

Cord and his chief designer, Gordon Buehrig, seemed to love. Continuing the themes of predecessor Al Leamy, Buehrig made the last Auburns even more flamboyant and aggressive, a look that did not translate perfectly from the speedsters to the sedans. Only 1200 Auburns sold in 1936.

Duesenberg was based upon an engine and an attitude. The engine, designed by Fred and August Duesenberg themselves, had the jewel-like precision of a Bugatti and put out 265 hp—about double that of any other production car. With a screaming 20,000-rpm supercharger, it was rated at 320 hp, more than any American car until 1956. The attitude was to harness this untamed racing

The one automotive project E. L. Cord seemed to make time for was the rebirth of his namesake auto, the Cord. First envisaged as a "Baby Duesenberg," the car's front-wheel drive led logically to reuse of the Cord badge. Gordon Buehrig was called in again to work his miracles. He sculpted the car in clay, using only his eye and rudimentary mechanical guides to shape the car's body, and in so doing redefined the form of the automobile for the next ten years.

1936

Shapes were simplified, with little chrome and minimal decoration. Headlights were hidden and the radiator grille became horizontal louvers set low around the squared-off hood. If ever there was a perfect dialogue between form and function, it is embodied in the "Coffin-Nosed Cord." Though the Cord's 1935 debut drew raves and copious orders, production delays and glitches limited sales to around 3000. As E. L. Cord's interests were diverted elsewhere, he divested himself of his auto properties, shutting down production of Auburn, Duesenberg, and finally Cord by August 1937.

1937
Adler Trumpf Stromlinie Coupe

Worldwide fascination with streamlining certainly affected automobile design as the thirties progressed. Racing aircraft, such as the American Gee-Bees and British Supermarine seaplanes, not to mention the new all-metal warplanes coming into service, introduced these exciting new forms to the public.

Aerodynamics was maturing as a science too. When the German firm of Adler raced at Le Mans in 1937, a lightweight, low-drag teardrop body was fitted over the very competent front-wheel-drive Trumpf Sport, which had a 70-hp, 1.7-liter, four-cylinder engine. Designed by aerodynamic engineer Karl Jenschke and coachbuilder Paul Jaray, who had just finished a similar design for Mercedes' Maybach, the long, low Trumpf Stromlinie finished first in its class and sixth overall in the 1937 Le Mans. Possibly the only survivor of the three race cars is shown at the Vuitton Concours in New York City.

1938 Delage D8-120 Speedster

With more of a tongue-in-cheek attitude toward the trappings of streamlining than a real attempt to lower wind resistance, this 1938 Delage D8-120 speedster takes a very French attitude to the world's obsession with the teardrop. The custom body by De Villers is actually one of the more restrained examples fitted to the grand 132-inch wheelbase D8 chassis with its 4-liter, 115-hp, straight-eight engine. Coachbuilding firms such as Saoutchik and Chapron dreamed up rococo barges, with overblown fenders and gobs of chrome that outdid American chariots right up until the early fifties. Other French makes, such as Talbot-Lago and Delage's stablemate Delahaye, received the same treatment.

This Delage, however, manages to preserve an elegant but masculine look, even while sporting its outrageous triple-tailed rear deck. It garnered three awards at the Lehigh, Pennsylvania, Concours in 1998.

1939 Heinz Phantom Corsair

A young boy listening intently to "The Shadow" or the "Green Hornet" radio programs back in the early forties, might have imagined his favorite super hero leaping into a car like this one. It is the Phantom Corsair, a one-of-a-kind fantasy designed by Rust Heinz of the wealthy "57 Varieties" family in 1938. Though his car looks sinister and more than a bit dangerous, the 23-year-old Heinz envisioned it as a safety vehicle. The wind-tunnel-tested body, built by Bowman and Schwartz, was fitted to a Cord 810 frame. Its Lycoming V-8 engine was boosted to 190 hp by up-and-coming race-car designer Andy Granatelli. Safety features included shatterproof glass, padded interior, and rear-facing passenger seats.

Heinz seriously considered limited production of the Corsair for 1939, to be priced at about $12,500, but he was killed (in a car crash) before any more were built. Appropriately enough, however, movie action hero Douglas Fairbanks, Jr., drove the car in a movie titled "The Young at Heart."

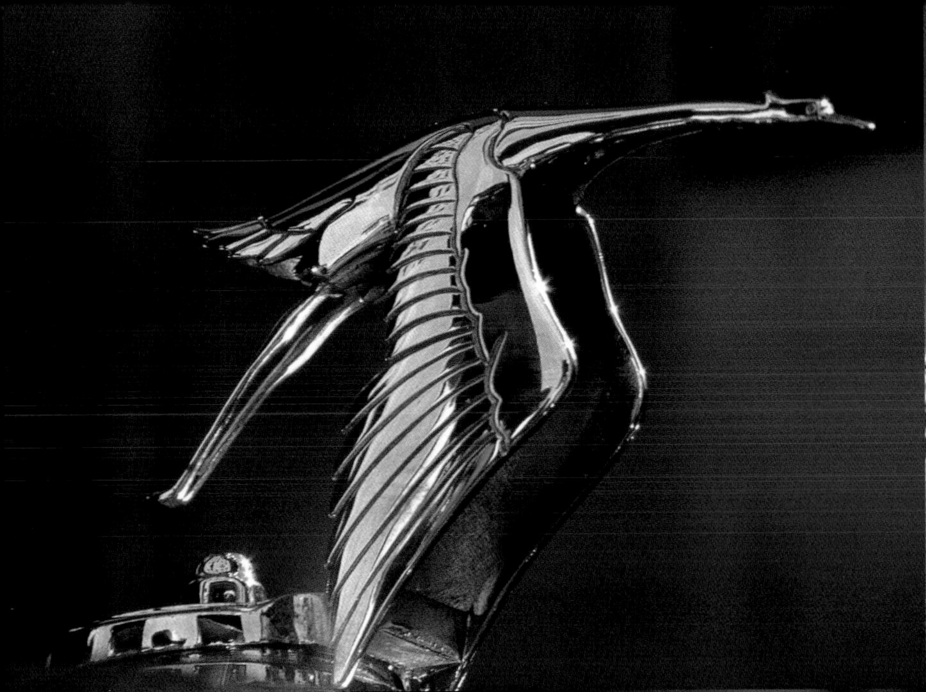

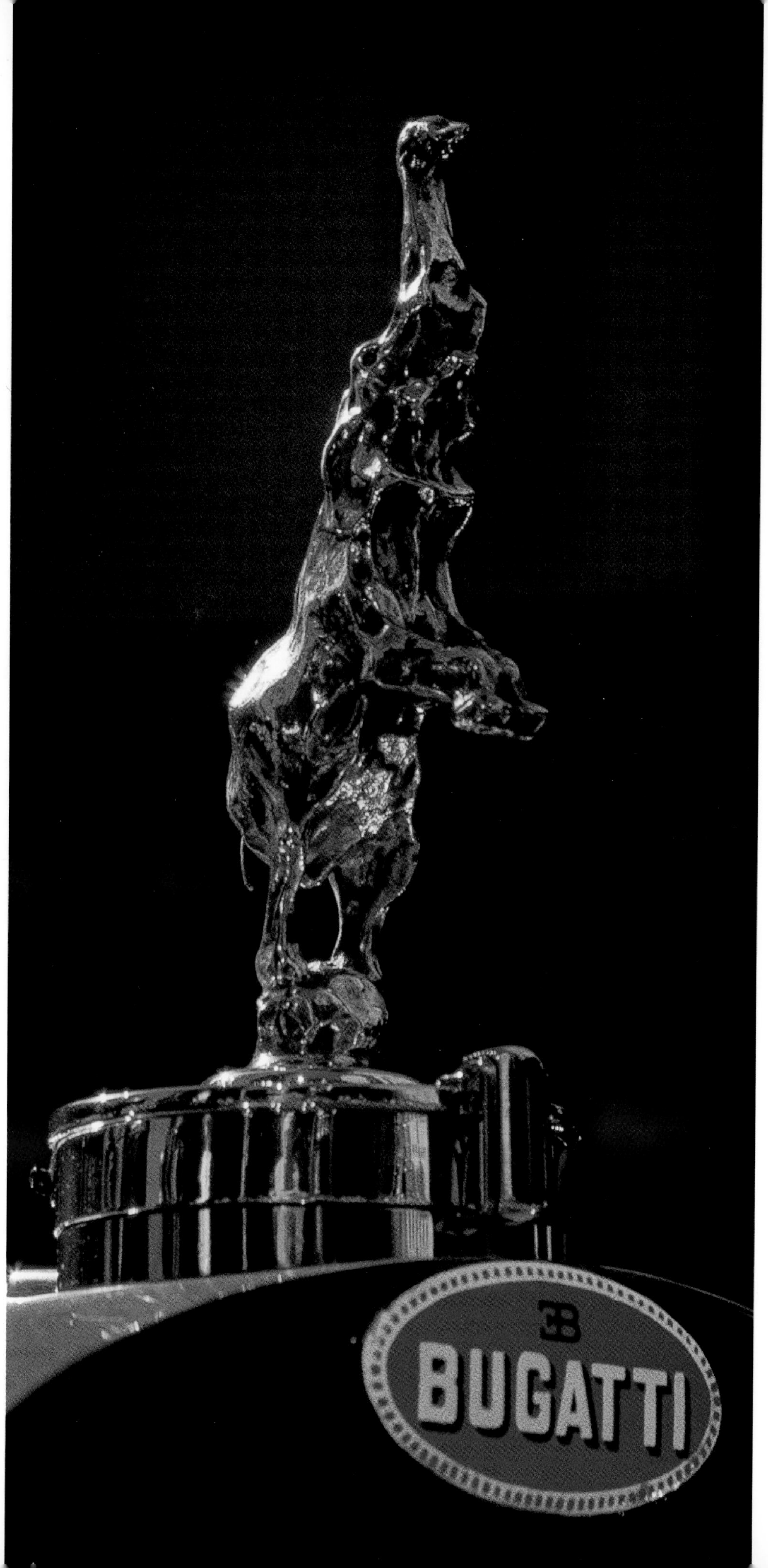

Radiator Mascots of the Classic Era

After radiators took their ordained place out in front of the engine of the early motorcar, their shapes were seen as unique marks of a car's identity. The radiator cap was merely a cap. A thermometer might be placed there, and these could be quite elaborate, with glass dials, twist-off handles, and even wings. But even as early as 1911, Rolls-Royce had commissioned artist Sir Charles Sykes to design a mascot or radiator sculpture known variously as "The Silver Lady," "The Spirit of Effortless Flight," or "The Spirit of Ecstasy." She is still with us.

By the mid-1920s, every make of car had a radiator ornament. Those machines—soon to be known as Classics—had, as was only fitting, the most elaborate and elegant of these miniature chrome sculptures. A Gallery of them is shown in this gatefold. European examples are the massive Bugatti Royale's elephant and the Hispano-Suiza's stork. Rudolph Valentino's Isotta Fraschini had his trademark "Viper" emblem. Just as well known in America were Pierce Arrow's archer, Packard's cormorant, Chrysler's gazelle, and Lincoln's greyhound. Stutz used the head of the sun goddess Ra. Later, in the thirties, ornaments grew more stylized and abstract like these Terraplane and Buick shapes illustrated.

Ornaments on foldout—top row, left to right:

Hispano-Suiza, Chrysler, Stutz, Isotta-Fraschini, Rolls-Royce, Pierce Arrow

Middle row, left to right:

Cadillac, Packard, Cadillac, Lincoln, Auburn

Bottom row, left to right:

Unknown, Packard, Duesenberg, Isotta-Fraschini, Buick, Terraplane

1940 Packard Darrin Convertible Sedan

A carelessly dropped ladies' straw hat evokes a soon-to-vanish era of fast touring in this swanky Packard straight-eight; war clouds seemed impossibly far off across the Atlantic in 1940. This was top-down driving at its best, and the couple owning this rare Darrin-bodied Packard still manage to put a few thousand miles a year on the car. The few paint nicks and chips that keep the car from serious concours competition are a small price to pay for the pleasure.

Packard, leery of the ostentatious, reluctantly gave in to dealer demands and produced a limited number of these models on the Custom Super-Eight body. Only 11 of the 1940 four-door models were sold at a price of $6300. Even though Packard was now looking toward the mid-price market, the drawing power of the flashy Darrin, also seen as a two-door Victoria, was undeniable. The already long hood grew another 18 inches but was 4 inches lower between voluptuous new fenders, and the windshield was sloped rakishly, the front doors cut down, and the running board eliminated. Shades of styling changes to come for tradition-bound Packard?

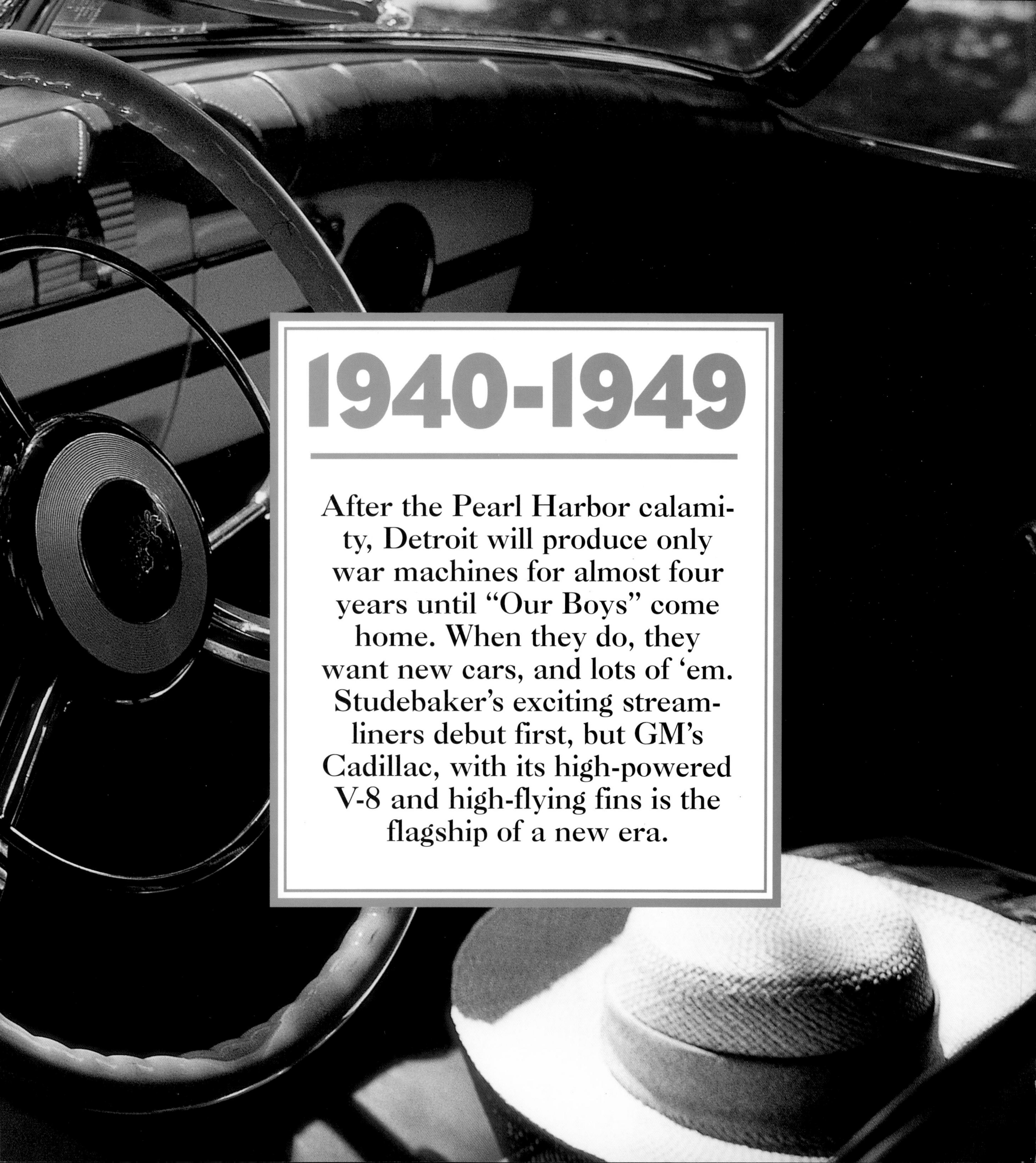

1940-1949

After the Pearl Harbor calamity, Detroit will produce only war machines for almost four years until "Our Boys" come home. When they do, they want new cars, and lots of 'em. Studebaker's exciting streamliners debut first, but GM's Cadillac, with its high-powered V-8 and high-flying fins is the flagship of a new era.

1941
Plymouth Staff Car

A Plymouth in khaki—an unsettling taste of the future as America, still hoping to stay out of war, becomes the "Arsenal of Democracy." A fatter military budget prompted the Army to impress 1500 top-of-the-line 1941 Plymouth Special Deluxe four-door sedans into service as staff transport. Plymouth was having a near-record year, though the car was not much changed from 1940. People were making good money at defense jobs now, and many guessed the chance to buy might not come again.

The Army chose well, as Plymouth was considered a rugged, inexpensive car. Since its introduction by Chrysler in 1928, Plymouth had clawed its way to third place behind only Ford and Chevy. This car's Pennsylvania owner believes it to be one of the original Army conscripts because when located in a used-car lot in the early seventies, it was in almost original condition, with olive-drab paint underneath its newer finish. The Plymouth has since been repainted with Army star and serial number and refitted with a siren.

1942
Packard Super Eight 180 Convertible Victoria

Returning to Packard for 1942, it was obvious that Howard "Dutch" Darrin acted as a catalyst for a momentous styling revolution underway at Packard. American-born Darrin came from a successful stint building custom bodies for Hispano and others in Paris. Returning to the United States in 1937, he settled in Hollywood, producing dream machines for stars such as Dick Powell.

Though this car is a 1942 Darrin Victoria model, almost all were sold in 1941, before the U.S. Government, reeling from Pearl Harbor, ordered all auto plants switched over to war production. Changes from the 1940 model previously shown derive mainly from the mid-price "Clipper" models introduced by Packard in April 1941. Darrin had been given ten days and $10,000 to come up with a proposal for the new Clipper. How much of the final production car was his is disputed, but it was unlike anything done before by Packard. This Super Eight 180 shows Clipper traits, such as the fender-mounted headlights and horizontal banding of the lower grille, while retaining the cut-down doors and beautifully appointed interior of previous Darrin Packards.

1943
Ford Air Corps Staff Car

No new cars! Detroit built not one automobile from spring 1942 until the end of 1945. This was perhaps the toughest of the hardships that American consumers endured during the war years, along with rationing, blackouts, and travel restrictions. Therefore, vehicles that served the U.S. armed forces will be used to illustrate those years.

This Air Corps staff car is a 1942 Ford "Fordor" sedan serving with the Eighth Air Force. Bumper markings place it with the 56th Fighter Group—the "Wolf Pack"—which flew P-47 Thunderbolts from English bases in 1943. A drab finish hides all the chrome trim of Ford's priciest model, the Super Deluxe. All Fords, however, sat upon the same 114-inch wheelbase and could be had with 96-hp V-8 or 90-hp six, and all had received a major facelift in 1942 with concealed running boards (finally!), larger grille, and generally more squared-off styling in keeping with its larger sibling, Mercury. But the Super Deluxe Ford had a more luxurious interior and sold for $45 more than the Deluxe. With wartime shortages, lower-quality materials were substituted for interior and exterior trim and engine parts as the truncated model year progressed.

1944
Dodge WC-52 Weapons Carrier

Pouring onto the beachhead in Normandy in the summer of 1944 were thousands of vehicles, from heavy tanks to small weapons carriers like this one. Built by Dodge and powered by their old reliable L-head six, the 3/4-ton-capacity, 98-inch-wheelbase workhorse was universally known as the "4 by 4" because of its four-wheel drive. The 1942 truck pictured here found its way to Norway after the war, remaining there until 1993, when it came to the United States. Charles Kern, a Pennsylvania resident, bought it in 1996. He has painted the Dodge in authentic U.S. Army markings, replaced the canvas top, and given it American tires and instruments. The Norwegians, he says, "kept the truck in good shape all these years."

America produced over 250,000 of these rugged machines between 1942 and 1945. They went to all war fronts and to our allies under Lend Lease agreements. Though not so beloved as the jeep, they were just as versatile, appearing as gun carriers, ambulances, and command vehicles.

HQ-9

1945

1945
Willys Jeep

This ferocious-looking jeep photographed at a Pennsylvania World War II re-enactment, bears the markings of the Ninth Air Force. Vehicles, such as these, with pedestal-mounted machine gun might have been seen guarding the B-26's of the 584th Squadron's forward air bases in France. In May 1945, victory came in Europe, thanks in part to the mobility granted to the G.I.'s by the go-anywhere jeep. Most jeeps were not as warlike as our example, but General Eisenhower hailed it as "one of the four weapons that won the war in Europe." Its official title was "Truck, Command Reconnaissance, 1/4 ton 4x4," and the jeep nickname might have come from a "Popeye" character. Besides serving as a scout car, the jeep could haul small artillery pieces and act as a litter carrier.

After the American Bantam Company, which had license-built the British Austin in the United States, created the prototype, production was given to Willys and Ford. During the war years, 600,000 were produced.

look and drove a postwar Continental for many years.

It was Edsel Ford who had wanted the light, understated look of the "continental" cars he had admired in Europe. Using the frame and V-12 engine from the Lincoln Zephyr, he had a long, low, special car built, and the attention it attracted around his Palm Beach home convinced him to start production. The 1940 and 1941 cars were primarily handbuilt machines. The Continental's engine was notoriously short-lived and underpowered, but in all other respects, from its pushbutton doors to its trademark rear-mounted spare, it was truly "the last of the classics."

1946
Postwar Lincoln Continentals

Many will argue that the postwar Continentals of 1946 through 1948 had lost the coherence and elegance of the original design. But these photos reveal the upright formality and solidity of these later models (this is a 1947) that carried on Continental's nascent classic tradition. Was the heavier, more horizontal design a reaction to GM and Chrysler's new models, where this look was acclaimed as more contemporary and futuristic? Probably, but Bob Gregorie, the Continental's chief designer, actually preferred the heavy

1947 Postwar Studebakers

Studebaker had been building vehicles since 1852, but they still considered themselves to be design leaders. They would be the first of the major automakers to get their radical new postwar cars into production. In the late thirties, they had brought aboard Raymond Loewy, one of the first true industrial designers and a great self-promoter, to style their cars, including the popular 1939 Champion. Though Loewy got credit for the 1947 Studebaker, it was Virgil Exner, later of Chrysler fame, who did the hands-on work. The car's eager, optimistic, forward-thrusting lines were a feast for the eyes of car-hungry motorists. This 1949 Champion Regal Deluxe convertible differs from the 1947 model in minor details, but it shows the horizontal grille and one-piece windshield that presaged the next ten years. Coupes were even more extreme, with wraparound rear windows and long rear decks.

However, styling seemed to be the whole story. Internally, Studebakers used the same engines and chassis as before the war, and, as other companies revealed their striking new models and the buyer's market evaporated, sales dropped disastrously.

1947-1948

1998
Concours d'Elegance
of the Eastern United States
1998
1948
CHRYSLER
EUGENE EPSTEIN
zymöl

1948 Chrysler Town and Country Convertible

The wood-paneled bodies of the Chrysler Town and Country models make them among the most collectible of postwar automobiles. Not bad for what is essentially a 1942 car. In fact the basic design dates from 1940, but consumer demand was still strong for almost any car Detroit could get out the door in 1948. Even with a price increase to $3500, almost 8400 sold. The beautifully hand-finished white-ash-and-mahogany bodywork, previously available only on station wagons, set them apart from other luxury cars. They were much in demand by Hollywood types, such as Marie McDonald and Leo Carillo.

Though the straight-eight engine was getting a bit long in the tooth, it soldiered on for another few years, giving the car that long-nosed classic hood of previous decades. A hydraulic-powered semiautomatic transmission added a modern touch. Fog lights and cowl-mounted spotlight were factory options, and nice, fat, white sidewalls cap the ensemble.

1949 Cadillac Series 62 Convertible

In 1948 Cadillac became the first GM car to receive sleek, new "postwar" bodies. The rear fenders sported twin fins or "fishtails" containing large plastic tail lamps. Though they served no aerodynamic purpose, they were inspired, we are told, by the twin rudders on the World War II Lockheed P-38 fighter plane. In 1949, the fins persisted, and Cadillac, not content with beginning the decade-long trend to ever-higher tail fins, inaugurated the "Horsepower Race" as well, with the introduction of their new 160-hp V-8 engine.

The 1949 series 62 convertible in our photos shows off the trim lines of that model even with the top up, which led to the debut that year of another revolutionary Cadillac model, the Coupe De Ville, or hardtop convertible. The other luxury carmakers—Packard, Lincoln, and Chrysler Imperial—even with their new postwar restylings, were hard pressed to keep up.

1950
Willys Jeepster

The wartime jeep returns, this time dressed in sporty "civvies." In 1948, Willys Overland Motors began selling their Jeepster, styled by industrial designer Brooks Stevens. Stevens added some chrome, whitewalls, and a sports-car-inspired convertible top with cut-down doors, while still keeping the military jeep's angular functional lines. There must have been plenty of nostalgic ex-G.I.s out there, because 10,000 were sold in the Jeepster's first year. Four-cylinder engines were standard at first, with a six being offered in 1949 and 1950. Willys, intent on introducing its new conventional-looking passenger cars, kept production of the Jeepster low and discontinued them altogether in 1951. The demand for used Jeepsters persisted, and the company, then owned by Kaiser, revived the brand in 1967. America's fascination with the sport utility vehicle had begun.

This Jeepster, a 1950 model, was bought new by a Connecticut artist who drives it to this day, preserved in mint condition.

1950-1959

A resurgent, confident America begins its dalliance with the British sporting car. Homegrown products pile on the sheet metal and the chrome to a Rock 'n Roll beat. Raymond Loewy's European-inspired Studebaker coupes set new design standards, and the Morris Mini virtually reinvents the small car.

74

1951
Allard PI Monte Carlo Coupe

America began a love affair with the sports car in the early fifties. Nothing like the European two-seat sports-touring car had been built in the United States for decades, and the Corvette, introduced in 1953, took a few years to mature. But British makes such as the MG and Jaguar offered an adventurous alternative to Detroit's cream puffs. The small Allard firm had its brief heyday because of a unique approach: using Ford-based components and V-8 engines, their race-proved cars were aimed toward American enthusiasts. Cadillac and Lincoln engines were available as well. With their big-engine acceleration they were "well nigh uncatchable" at rallies and on winding roads. A Cadillac-powered Allard took third at Le Mans in 1950. Bodies were of two types: the "K" model, looking oh so British with teardrop fenders and flat windscreen, and the racing "J" model with cycle fenders, stand-alone headlights, and cut-down doors.

Here though is an Allard of a different sort, the Monte Carlo Coupe, a two-door model not intended for export. It retained the sporty front-end styling and Ford V-8 engine of the American-targeted cars, but added some niceties such as a closed top with roll-up windows and air conditioning. Only 337 Allards were sold in 1951.

1952
Nash Healey Le Mans Racer

The race to capitalize on the U.S. sports-car rage spawned some remarkably strange partnerships. Perhaps the oddest was the Nash Healey, product of a chance ocean-voyage meeting between Nash president George Mason and Donald Healey, British maker of sporting cars. Mason was looking for a way to add spice to his stodgy company, and Healey, perhaps emulating Allard, wanted big American V-8's for his autos. The result, with a dash of Italian design flair added, was an exotic sports car indeed.

This particular Nash Healey looks ready to race. The staid old Nash Kelvinator coat of arms clashes with the businesslike white-on-silver racing numbers. Still, the 4-liter Nash Ambassador, a Dual-Jetfire-Six-powered car, finished an amazing third at Le Mans in 1952. The no-nonsense slab-sided body with headrest was gentrified a bit in its production version, with body by Pinin Farina and a chrome-heavy grille. They were real sports cars, but Nash lost money on every one and by 1954 had shifted focus to more prosaic economy cars.

1953 Aston Martin DB Series

This study in slate gray epitomizes the understated, very British elegance possessed by Aston Martin sports cars of the fifties and sixties. The company struggled in the early post-war years, despite a proud racing heritage, until the advent of new owner David Brown, who besides money and expertise, lent his initials to a new series of sporting cars. The DB2 exemplified Aston Martin's new vitality: a 2.6-liter, twin-cam six using Lagonda (now also owned by Brown) design experience, a racing-type tubular chassis with coil spring on all four wheels, and a curvaceous body designed by Frank Feeley, previously a stylist for Lagonda. In the 1954 DB2/4, Feeley elevated the rear roof line of the fastback DB2 to add two more passenger seats, thereby creating one of the first sports hatchbacks. Note that the rear window and trunk lid are combined to give access to the rear area. Interior appointments, though spartan by American standards, were exceedingly well crafted.

Incremental redesign over the years led to the 1964 DB5, immortalized as James Bond's mount in *Goldfinger,* and the V-8-powered DBS in 1969, the last of the DB models.

1954 Studebaker Champion Starlight Two-Door

If the post-war Studebaker had been a breath of fresh air, the 1953 "Loewy Coupes" were works of art. The dramatic new Starliner hardtop was the only American car in the Museum of Modern Art's "Ten Automobiles" exhibit in New York that year. Bob Bourke of Raymond Loewy's staff had adopted the look of European touring coupes, such as the Cisitalia and the Ferrari, in the long (120-inch wheelbase) and low (56.5 inches high) machine. Using "faster" curves than the more rounded contours favored by GM and other manufacturers gave the impression that the sheet metal was stretched tautly over the body. Forms were kept simple, with chrome minimized and glass area maximized. But demand for the hardtops could not be met. Production teething troubles and antiquated plants kept sales low.

The 1954 models, such as this Starlight two-door coupe, were virtually unchanged except for vertical "teeth" in the grille openings and squared-off bumper guards. The design was very adaptable—and a good thing too—for it soldiered on in various forms until Studebaker's demise ten years later.

1955

1955 Chevrolet Del Ray Two-Door Sedan

In a time when pink and black were *the* fashion colors, and chrome dripped from American cars, the 1955 Chevy seems a model of restraint. Harley Earl and the stylists at GM had all new body and sheet metal to work with, but they kept their basic design simple and clean. Styling cues borrowed from Cadillac were used to suggest class and quality: the "frenched" headlights, the egg-crate grille (which Earl maintained was a Ferrari touch), the long, straight rear fenders. The "panoramic" windshield and notched beltline—a vestigial reminder of the vanished rear fender—were shared with all GM cars. New also for 1955 was a long-overdue V-8 engine, the overhead-valve "Turbofire" block, that helped push sales into overdrive—1.7 million Chevrolets sold that year.

The Del Ray (aka the Two-Ten) sedan illustrated is a contemporary custom—mild outside, wild inside. Owner Walt Helstocki installed a rolled and pleated 1970 Chevelle interior into the Strawberry Red two-door. Its 1970 engine now pumps out 418 hp and 500 pounds/foot of torque.

1956 Buick Super Riviera Two-Door Hardtop

The 1956 Buick parked in the breezeway of your split-level home told a lot about you. Any savvy person could read the totemic symbols imprinted in your cars brightwork. First of all, you had style, for the Buicks of that year were quite elegant and well proportioned, a refinement of the "million dollar grin" Buicks of the early fifties, but not yet showing the excesses of the overweight bulgemobiles of 1957 and 1958. You were also a bit sporty, choosing a two-tone hardtop, with a cutaway rear-wheel opening and signature "sweepspear." Last, you were well off—the Buick was just below Caddy in the GM line-up and the four-porthole Super was just below the grand Roadmaster. Other Buick symbols echoed the times: jet-intake bumper guards, sweptwing hood ornament, and gullwing grille emblem all denoted your love of speed and power, both of which the Buick could deliver—100 mph and 255 hp. The fact that the car was comfortable transportation seemed beside the point. GM read the market well; 570,000 were sold, and Buick held onto third place.

Super

1957 Chevrolet Bel Air Convertible

Why has the 1957 Chevy become a Fabulous Fifties icon like Elvis and the hula hoop? It was a good car, but Plymouth and Ford had new bodies and were longer, wider, and lower than Chevrolet's facelifted 1955. The magnificent Chevy V-8 had been bored out to 283 potent cubic inches, but Plymouth and Ford had new engines too. In fact, Ford fought Chevy to a standstill in sales numbers.

So why is the 1957 Chevy the quintessential fifties car? Because it is cool. Cool like a kid in sunglasses and leather jacket. Not taking itself too seriously, saying: "I've got chrome, I've got fins, I've got a fuel-injected 283 engine, dual exhausts, a copper metallic paint job, and hood scoops. What've you got?" It was meant to be basic transportation, the low-price leader from GM. But to the average Joe who would spend from $1800 to $3500 for one it was a mini-Cadillac. It was an instant custom and an instant classic. When all the Plymouths had rusted out and the Fords had faded in the glow of the Thunderbird, the 1957 Chevy was, and still remains, the most popular used car ever. Wanna drag?

Chevrolet
Bel Air

States, as it was affordable—under $4000, very roadworthy, and at the time the fastest production car available, with a twin overhead-cam engine producing 160 hp. The white grille detail, black coupe, and red-tailed convertible are 120s. The red coupe shown, an XK-140, debuted in 1955. It kept the time-honored lines but beefed-up bumpers and chrome trim, as well as the engine—now up to 190 hp. In 1958, the last update of the series appeared. The black convertible (or "drophead coupe" in British parlance) is the XK-150. Lines were more rounded and smoothed, and a one- piece windscreen was provided, along with a roomier, more luxurious interior. Engine options could produce as much as 250 hp.

1958 Jaguar XK Series Sports Cars

Leave it to the British to make a virtue out of anachronism. The XK series Jaguars were lovely machines, but the body designs, by William Lyons, with swooping fenders and upright radiator grilles were redolent of the Classic Era. They were powered by six-cylinder engines when V-8's seemed the way to go. Oddly, entry on the roadsters was solely by means of little leather straps inside the doors. Americans couldn't get enough of them.

Our pictures are a compendium of three generations of XK cars. In 1948 came the XK-120 (named after its top speed), a sensation in the United

1959 JAG
PENNSYLVANIA

1959 Austin and Morris Minis

Yes, it is the kind of car that Mr. Bean drives, and, yes, we know this is a 1967 Mini Cooper S, but it was in 1959 that this revolutionary little car was born. As heir to the diminutive British Austin "Seven," the new model 850 virtually reinvented the automobile. It was designer Alec Issigonis' inspiration to mount the 52-cubic-inch, four-cylinder engine crosswise under the hood, allowing very spacious seating in a car less than 120 inches long. Austin and Morris produced versions of the cars concurrently; Riley and Wolsely variants also appeared.

The gutsy, functional design won numerous awards and inspired a quest for hotter performance. So in 1963, with the help of John Cooper, the Mini Cooper and later Mini Cooper S emerged. Engines in these later models range from 1000 cc and 55 hp up to 1275 cc and 75 hp—quite potent for a 1300-pound car. Though the Mini was never the success in the United States that it was (and still is) worldwide, many of the small American cars to come adopted the transverse-engine layout.

1960 Chevrolet Impala Two-Door Hardtop

As the best-selling car in the United States, Chevrolet had led the trend toward bigger and fancier low-priced cars. But stylewise, Chevy seemed to flounder. An all-new 1958 body was dumped in 1959 for an exotic fantasy known for its gullwing fins and "cats-eye" tail lights. The 1960 facelift toned things down some with squared-off rear fins and a simpler grille. The 1961 cars were still more restrained, but full-size Chevys continued to balloon until by 1974 they rode on a 121.5-inch wheelbase and were 18.5 feet long! During this time the Chevrolet division spawned a whole stable of compacts, sub-compacts, and mid-sized cars to fill the gap as Chevy morphed into a "full-sized car."

This almost-factory-stock 1960 Chevrolet is a top-tier Impala model owned by Bob Kane, Jr., who likes the hardtop's "bubble top" roof line and special hound's-tooth upholstery. Its engine is the much-loved 283 V-8 with Powerglide.

1960-1969

Power! The sixties are about power. If power corrupts, what about horsepower? In European cars, power is embodied in the sensual 300 SL and the XK-E. In the United States, more is more: monster engines, screaming superchargers, gaping air scoops. It is the age of the muscle car.

1961

1961 Jaguar XK-E

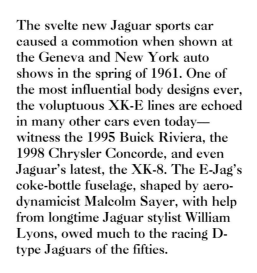

The svelte new Jaguar sports car caused a commotion when shown at the Geneva and New York auto shows in the spring of 1961. One of the most influential body designs ever, the voluptuous XK-E lines are echoed in many other cars even today—witness the 1995 Buick Riviera, the 1998 Chrysler Concorde, and even Jaguar's latest, the XK-8. The E-Jag's coke-bottle fuselage, shaped by aerodynamicist Malcolm Sayer, with help from longtime Jaguar stylist William Lyons, owed much to the racing D-type Jaguars of the fifties.

Under the sensuously curved body was the powerful 265-hp, 3.8-liter six from the XK-150 on a space-frame-type front frame mated to a monocoque or unit body. A speed of 150 mph was claimed. The roadster pictured here is a 1966 model, but it differed little from the originals, except for a larger 4.2-liter engine. Also new that year was a longer, roomier 2+2 coupe that could be had with automatic transmission. XK-E production ceased in 1975.

30
40
50
60
70
20
10
RPM
x100
UPM
VDO
80
60
100
120
140
20
0
MPH
VDO
48001
FUEL

1962 Mercedes-Benz 300SL Roadster

This was the penultimate year for the immortal 300SL. When introduced in 1954 as a 1955 model, it caused as much furor, especially in "gullwing" coupe form, as the XK-E did in 1961. Developed from the sensational 300SL Le Mans cars, which finished one, two, three in 1952, the new Mercedes used a race-car-type, tubular "space frame" rather than the traditional flat chassis members. The frame enclosed engine and passengers and supported the body components, necessitating high door sills; hence the gullwing doors pivoted at the roof, as did the much later DeLorean. Once inside the cabin, creature comforts were top level. A 3-liter, six-cylinder engine from the sedan was used, turning out 240 hp through the use of the first-ever production fuel-injection system. Speed and acceleration set new standards.

This 1962 SL roadster differs little from the soft-top model introduced to replace the gullwing in 1957, except for handling improvements and more power. When the 230SL appeared in 1963, its disappointing "pagoda roof" styling made enthusiasts realize that nothing could replace the 300SL.

1963 Chevrolet Bel Air Custom Rod

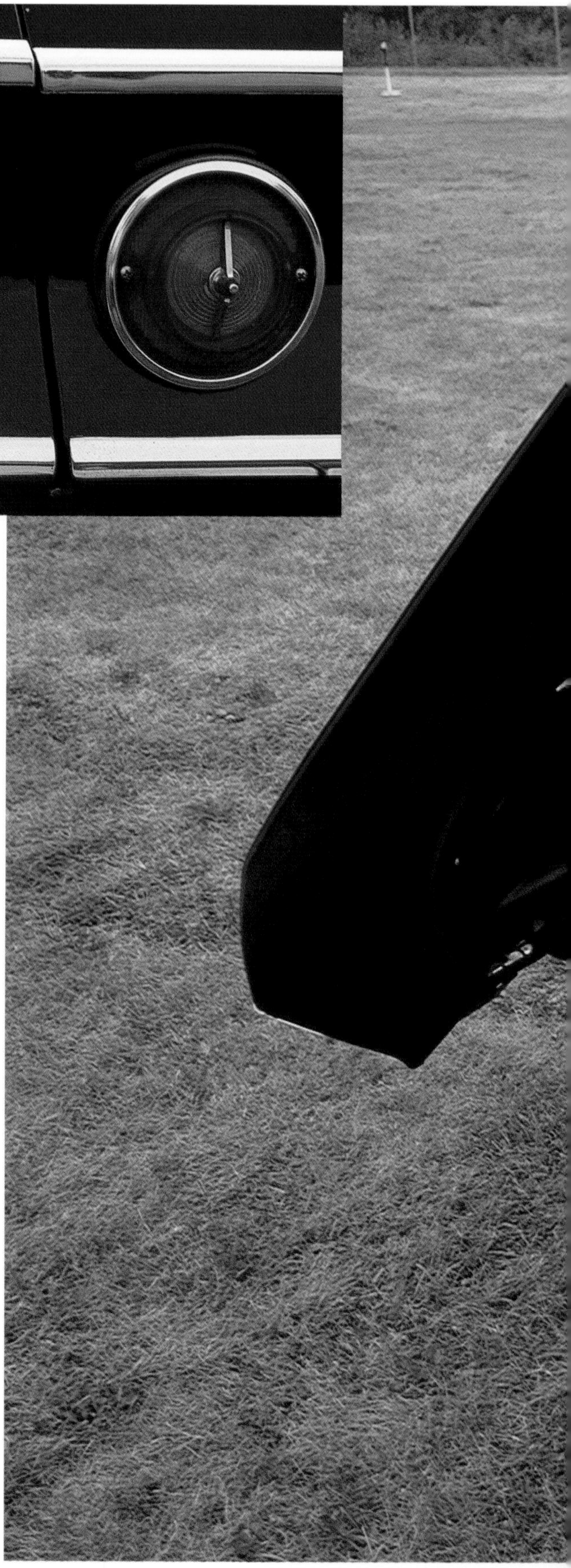

Take a standard 1963 Chevy—a nice-looking if mild-mannered kind of a car, ideal for the suburban family—and gut the front end. Remove the front bumpers, and combine hood and fenders into a flip-top front end in the style of a racing Jaguar. Under that hood is, we believe, a 1970 Chevrolet engine. Could it be the legendary 454-cubic-inch monster that first became available that year as a performance option on the new Monte Carlo? We

just don't know, having lost touch with the owner, but we do know that this Chevy has been in the family since it was new. Chevrolet offered a lightweight front end as a racing option that accomplished much the same thing as seen here, though this custom Bel Air emphasizes the already exaggerated short hood and long rear deck of GM cars of the time.

Along with the sinister black-and-chrome look are rather risqué etched-glass vent wings that only add to the subtle S&M quality of the machine. No more family car, this.

BFGoodrich
Radial T/A

1964
Studebaker Avanti Sport Coupe

A last desperate gesture from a doomed company, and the last auto design from the Raymond Loewy studios, produced one of the truly original cars of the century—the Avanti. Studebaker's new president, Sherwood Egbert, gave Loewy just 13 months to produce a prototype. As in 1953 the design staff turned to Europe for inspiration. A short, uptilted rear deck, "coke bottle" nipped-in waist, and long razor-edged nose evoked Italian GT cars. The forward rake and underslung intake scoop suggested a performance machine, and a supercharged V-8 was available. But this was a true five-passenger car, built, in fact, on the old Lark chassis. Fiberglass was chosen for quick production, but this backfired, and delays meant only 3800 1963 Avantis were made.

The 1964 model, recognizable by its square headlights, fared even worse. Studebaker finished only 800 before shutting down U.S. operations and moving to Canada for a short respite before the end, though the Avanti would continue in production in private hands through the 1980s.

1965
Ford Thunderbird Landau

Having long ago lost any claim to being a sports car when it became the four-seater in 1958, the Thunderbird was still a unique car. Neither GM nor Chrysler matched it in their mid-size ranges. It sat on the wheelbase of cars like the Chevelle or Dodge Polara, yet looked much bigger, more like the Buick Riviera or the still-to-come Toronado, and it was priced to match.

The brand-new Ford Mustang took aim at the "youth market" for an inexpensive, sporty personal car. But its big brother the T'Bird would get you noticed. It was flashy and flamboyant, and a little over the top. Even the standard engine put out a solid 300 horses, with a "super high performance" 427-cubic-inch mill available for the speed-deprived. Simulated landau irons on a black vinyl top over a Cherry Red finish added a certain something, and bringing up the rear were those huge, chrome-encased, sequentially flashing tail lights that left no doubt as to your turning intentions.

New Jersey
65BIRD
HISTORIC

1966 Ford GT 40 Marks I to IV

This was the year that Ford got truly serious about racing. The goal was the World Sports Car Manufacturers Championship, and the GT 40 racer was the means. Development began in 1962 when Ford announced a commitment to "Total Performance," and, in a cooperative effort with British Ford, some rear-engined Mustang ideas grew into the GT 40 (named, strangely enough, for its height). The car was low and aerodynamic, its sinuous curves designed by John Wyer, late of Aston Martin, and Eric Broadley of Lola GT fame, using wind-tunnel models. At first powered by U.S.-supplied 289 V-8's, the British-built Mark I showed promise,

but Le Mans attempts in 1964 and 1965 were abortive.

With the 7-liter, 429-engined Mark II of 1966, everything seemed to gel. Now came the victories: Daytona, Sebring, and, at last, Le Mans, where the cars finished first, second, and third in a much-publicized "formation finish." Ford swept Le Mans again in 1967 and 1968 with drivers like Dan Gurney and A. J. Foyt, and cars much like this 1967 Mark IV.

1967 Chevrolet Camaro RS Convertible

Memorial Day, 1967. Leading the racers at the Indianapolis 500 as official pace car is Chevrolet's entry in the "pony car" derby, the Camaro. Sharing a body with Pontiac's new Firebird, Camaro was part of GM's two-prong attack on the Ford Mustang, creator of the new small-personal-car category. Since Mustang's debut in mid-1964, almost a million and a quarter had been sold. GM needed a slice of that pie.

Camaro styling was clean and curvy, versus Mustang's edgy slab-sided design, though both came in 2+2 coupe and convertible models and both rode the same 108-inch wheelbase. But Camaro's gimmick was the endless option packages offered, a buyer's custom-car wish book. The Rally Sport model, pictured here, was the first rung up the ladder from the plain-vanilla six that nobody bought . Along with "RS" trim options and concealed headlights, you'd want the 327 V-8 engine, four on the floor, and a posi-traction rear. In the muscle-car class was the popular 350-cube SS, the Trans-Am-derived Z-28, and even a replica of that Indy pace car. Docile or muscle-bound, you could roll your own, and Chevy's pony car looked to be a winner.

1968 Bizzarrini P-538 Racer

Fate decreed that this Bizzarrini would not run at Le Mans in 1968. Rule changes meant that the beautiful Lamborghini-powered racer no longer met the "homologation," or production, qualifications. Giotto Bizzarrini's struggling firm never recovered from the blow. He had started out with Ferrari in 1957, his creative talents contributing much to the company, including primary design responsibility for the brilliant Ferrari 250 GT. Clashes with Enzo Ferrari led to his striking out on his own with consultant projects for Lamborghini and the Iso company. With Lamborghini, he worked on the V-12 engine that still powers the company's machines. For Iso, he was involved in producing the Iso Grifo, some modifications of which were built under his own name and called the Strada. In 1965, Bizzarrini envisioned a new design, the rear-engined Corvette-powered P-538, with fiberglass body styled by Giugiaro. An open-cockpit version of the car competed unsuccessfully at Le Mans in 1966.

After his company's supposed break-up, it seems that Bizzarrini, his wife, and a few workers actually hand-assembled some cars from parts on hand. This is one such, chassis Number 002, the planned Le Mans racer, owned by Van Horneff, a Saddle River, New Jersey, man who keeps the unique car in racing condition.

1969 Ford Mustang GT Convertible

The car that started the pony-car stampede got a new body this year. Still on the same 108-inch wheelbase, the 'Stang was longer and huskier looking, with plenty of room under the hood for some big iron. The all-out performance race of the late sixties was hotting up, and Mustang faced serious competition from Camaro and others.

These Mustangs are serious collectibles now and are being "restored" to factory condition. Conscious of this, Ed Moreno, owner of this 351 GT, has since replaced its aftermarket steering wheel with original equipment. Though the four-barrel, 10.7:1-compression, 290-hp engine could move, it was only the start for muscle Mustangs. Next up was the Code S 390 GT, then the legendary Mach 1 and Boss Mustangs, which could be had with the awesome 429-cubic-inch engine, a beast that put out almost 500 hp. Lee Iacocca's vision of Mustang as a stylish personal car had been co-opted by Ford CEO Bunkie Knudsen, whose obsession with competition and performance was legendary.

1970 Oldsmobile Cutlass S Rallye 350

The fading light of an upstate New York summer evening does little to dim the high-visibility Sebring Yellow finish of the 1970 Cutlass Rallye 350. Enthusiastically restored by Charley and Kathy Scott, it is one of only 2500 built. Offered solely in 1970, the specially finished Oldsmobile came with fiberglass hood scoops, rear spoiler, and some of the first urethane plastic bumpers, as well as a 350-cubic-inch, 310-hp engine.

Like almost all mid-size cars of this time, Oldsmobile was trying—successfully—to goose sales with a "muscle car" performance image. Olds was emulating GM's Pontiac division, which, under the guidance of John DeLorean, took the bloodless Tempest and forged it into the GTO, the first muscle car to be marketed as such, in 1963. The most-renowned of Olds muscle cars were the 4-4-2's (the numbers stood for 4 carburetors, 4-speed shift, and dual exhausts). Less well known were the "W-machines" and the longer-lived Hurst/Olds cars. Certainly a far cry from, and 12 million cars later than, that first curved-dash Olds of 1901.

1970-1979

The industry is brought low, drained of its life blood by successive oil crises. Now small is beautiful. Japan, a master of the small and understated, starts its climb with sure-footed machines like the Land Cruiser. But the big guys—Cadillac and Mercedes—wait patiently in the wings.

1971 Triumph TR Series Sports Cars

Even at the height of muscle-car madness in 1971, there remained a coterie of driving enthusiasts who craved the song of a close-ratio gearbox, the thrill of a controlled drift in a tight turn, wind in their hair. All this and more the Triumph TR6 could provide, and at half the price of a Jaguar XK-E.

Introduced in 1969, the TR6 was the latest in a line of Triumph two-seaters begun with the 1954 TR2, a no-frills, rough-riding, but gutsy little car.

Evolving from its original bug-eyed look through Italian designer Giovanni Michelotti's TR4 into the civilized, contemporary-looking TR6 restyled by Germany's Karmann with a now obligatory cut-off rear end or "Kamm-back." The 1971 racing season under the aegis of the Sports Car Club of America was for Triumph a real eye-opener. After TR6's early success in regional racing for 1969 and 1970, the new Datsun 240Z was proving impossible to beat. Lessons learned from SCCA experience were applied to the 1973 TR6 shown here. The most prominent addition was the under-bumper front air dam, but exhaust valves and overdrive also saw modifications.

1973 Plymouth 'Cuda Hardtop

This might be "one bad fish," but unless there are some surprise goodies under that twin-scoop hood, this 1973 'Cuda might be a sardine swimming with the sharks. In that year of the Oil Crisis, muscle-car gas guzzlers were dead in the water. Gone were the big 'Cuda engines, especially the superb Hemi, Chrysler's legendary performance mill, along with the 383, the 440, and all the underhood options, except for a mediocre 235-hp, twin-carb V-8. But they still looked mean, and 10,000 were sold.

Gone were the glory years of 1970 and 1971, when monsters like *Nash Bridges* star Don Johnson's 1971 Hemi 'Cuda topped the food chain. Derived from the Plymouth Barracuda—you knew that!—which was, in turn, a fastback Valiant, the 'Cuda joined the stable of Plymouth muscle cars, such as the GTX, the Duster, and the (beep-beep!) Road Runner, all casualties of Detroit's downsizing in the seventies. It was time to think about gas mileage, catalytic converters, and crashworthy bumpers.

1972 Alfa Romeo 2000 Spider Veloce

The 1972 Alfa Romeo brochure called its new 2000-series cars "race refined," and so they were. Since 1911, Alfa had made its reputation on the race course with cars like the 1924 P2 and the immortal 1750 models, as well as the otherworldly "disco volante" of 1952, and the 1971 33/3. Champion drivers' names, such as Nuvolari and Fangio, would forever be tied to the name of Alfa Romeo.

The 2000 Spider pictured was refined in other ways as well. The jewel-like fuel-injected double-overhead-cam engine had been bored out to 2 liters and now delivered 129 hp. The interior was luxurious, with reclining leather seats and wood steering wheel, and the body design by Pinifarina had been newly restyled with cut-off Kamm-back. Further refinements kept the Spider and its descendants in production almost 20 years more. In 1985, a lower-priced version called "The Graduate" memorialized Dustin Hoffman's Alfa in that 1967 movie.

NEW YORK
1BADFISH

'cuda 340

1974 Volkswagen Karmann-Ghia Cabriolet

Not only would 1974 be the last year for the Karmann-Ghia, but by the end of the next year, the ageless VW Beetle also began to leave the scene with only the quaint convertible hanging around until 1979. Volkswagen remained a vital world-class company, however, producing cars such as the Rabbit, which were perfect for their time.

The Karmann-Ghia had no close U.S. rivals when it came to America in 1956. It was a stylish and, more importantly, a low-priced 2+2 sporty car for those who didn't want the commitment of owning a sports car and couldn't see themselves at the wheel of a clunky, bare-bones VW Bug. Though the car used the frame and drive train of the Beetle (for that matter so did the original Porsche), styling was by the fashionable Ghia of Italy, and coachwork was by Germany's Karmann. The 1974 Cabriolet seen here shows very little exterior change from the 1956 originals, and that oddly long-tailed look still holds up well today. Later entries in this class, such as the Corvair Monza, were usually much higher powered. Renault's 1959 Caravelle seemed a near match, but, while styled with Gallic flair, it had disappeared by 1968.

1975 Chevrolet Caprice Convertible

It was truly "The Last Convertible," at least for the full-size Chevrolet. Nine years elapsed before the next ragtop Chevy. In 1984 the Cavalier met the challenge of the new Chrysler LeBaron. This 1975 Caprice nostalgia-mobile took a more delicate approach to chrome than the 1950s cars it recalled, but still rode a Cadillac-sized wheelbase and weighed 4300 pounds. Boxy aircraft-carrier-like front and rear decks went on forever. Wasn't this just what America had ordered for so many years? Now though, Federal emission controls were in place, and new gas consumption standards were about to take effect. The 1975 Chevies had catalytic converters and "5 mph" bumpers, but the new downsized models took time

to move from concept to production; they would not appear until 1977. Meanwhile there was a menagerie of Chevrolets to choose from in 1975. Besides the Caprice there was the Monte Carlo, Nova, Chevelle, Vega, Monza, and Camaro, not to mention the inimitable Corvette. Each one was a totally different automobile.

1976 Toyota Land Cruiser 40 Series

In this Bicentennial year, America's auto industry seemed to be under assault from all sides. Symbolic of the "enemy" in some of its forms is this seemingly tranquil brand-new Land Cruiser. The Japanese auto onslaught was building, as was the trend toward smaller vehicles (even trucks). America's rediscovery of nature and the great outdoors brought a newly felt need for huskier, more competent off-the-road vehicles. Only Jeep, then owned by American Motors, was partially meeting this need and was thereby keeping the struggling automaker going.

Designed to much the same specs as the World War II jeep, the first Land Cruiser of 1950 was quite a bit larger and heavier, with a 3.4-liter six. Early Land Cruisers reached U.S. shores in 1958. These were model 25's, a military-looking pickup or wagon with four-wheel drive. The classic Series 40 removable hardtop/soft top shown here was built from 1961 until 1984, and for a while, it outsold every other Toyota. By 1976 they had a larger 4.2-liter engine, power-disk brakes, and four-speed transmission. Today's models are loaded with options but can still tow three tons or more. More than 250,000 have been sold.

1977 Mercedes 450 SEL 6.9 Sedan

Looks like just another top-of-the-line Mercedes S-Class sedan, an expensive and luxurious autobahn cruiser. But the numerals "6.9" discreetly affixed to the trunk lid signal the presence of a 6.9-liter engine under the hood and makes this Mercedes something special. It was called the "Bankers' Hot Rod." To *Road and Track* magazine it was "the fastest, best sedan in the world." As the U.S. began driving four-cylinder "econo-boxes," Daimler Benz offered the car almost reluctantly to American buyers, who snapped up 500 almost instantly. Even detuned for the U.S. market, the engine gave 250 hp and topped 130 mph. The 6.9's other major goody was the "hydropneumatic" suspension for effortless handling. American 6.9's like this one had big, black rubber bumpers and quad headlights. Leather and wood adorned the interior, yet even allowing for the car's age, the cockpit seems austere for its 1977 price of $40,000. Seats are manual, as are the mirrors, and the shifter is awkward, but forget all that. Just floor it, and you'll empty that 25-gallon tank in no time.

1978
Cadillac Coupe deVille

The era of hard-edge styling, formal hardtops, and opera windows was upon us. Cadillac was one of the few cars able to carry off that look, an example being this vinyl-roofed 1978 DeVille. For Cadillac's Diamond Anniversary in 1977, the DeVille had been downsized, losing 1000 pounds, and the giant 500-cubic-inch engine. (Was nothing sacred?) Gone also were the convertibles. But Caddy carried on serenely to its third record year, helped by the popular new Seville models. And the latest engine, the high-torque 7-liter V-8, still gave ample performance.

This original-condition Coupe deVille wears its twenty-plus years well, showing off the Dunlop wire wheels, offered for 1978 in a short-lived revival, and of course its understated but seemingly eternal fins. The red leather interior has worn quite well, but the acres of fake wood now look dated. Speaking of dated, topping the options list for 1978 were a CB radio and eight-track tape player!

1979
Porsche 935

Under all that racing finery, behind the massive front air dam, beneath the rear spoiler and the double-wide rear-fender scoops, beats the heart of a Porsche 911. The 911, Porsche's mainstay since its debut in 1963/1964 was a capable sports car in road or racing form, but here it had mutated into something more. The most amazing of a whole series of 935 racers

were the turbocharged 3.2-liter K versions. These brutes produced up to 800 hp and could go from 0 to 60 mph in 3.3 seconds. The 935 shown here, owned by the Brumos Collection and class winner at the 1998 Vuitton Concours in New York City, won the American IMSA championship in 1979. It is all original, down to driver Peter Gregg's Scottish tartan seat cover. The 935's, based however remotely on production cars, enabled Porsche to win the Production Car Championship three years running—1977 through 1979—capping it all with the 1979 Le Mans win. The somewhat more sedate 911 was manufactured in various guises until 1997 when it was replaced by a new 911 for the millennium, the Carrera.

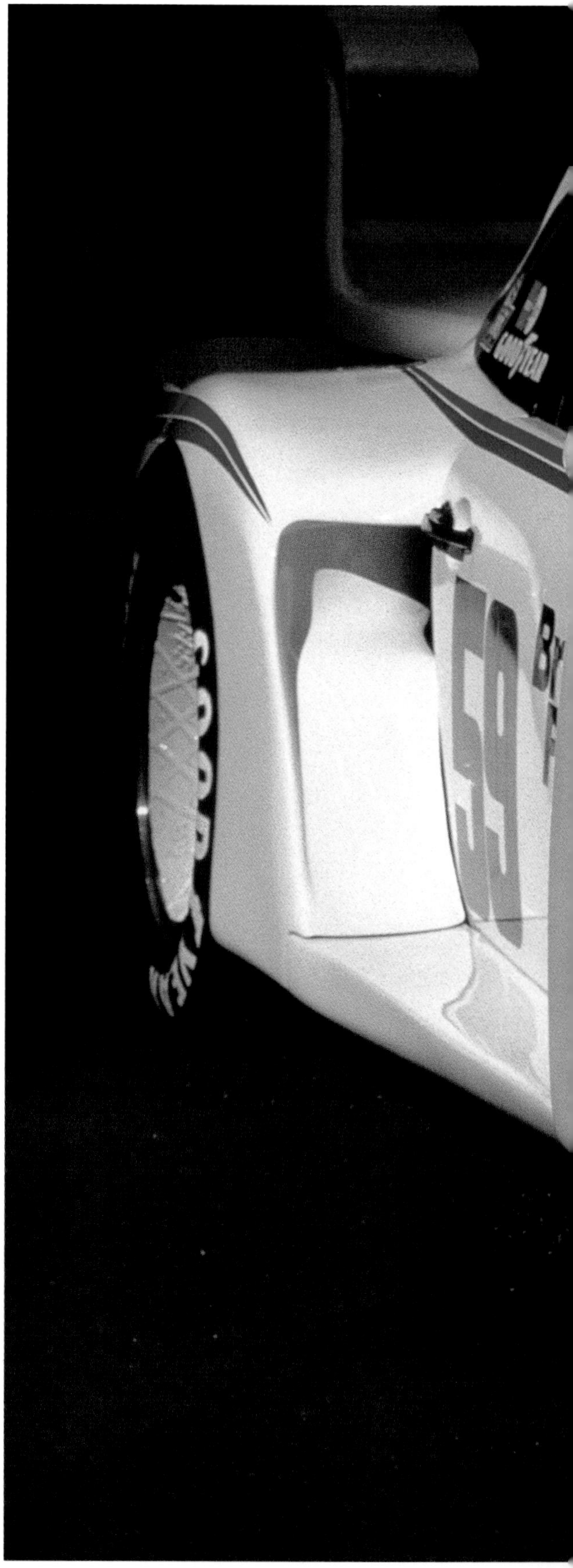

Brumos Porsche
GOODYEAR
59
Brumos Po
BOSCH
Kendall

1980 BMW M-1 Sports Coupe

Possibly an odd choice to represent BMW for the eighties, since it resembles no other "Beemer" before or since, this was BMW's entry in the "supercar" sweepstakes. And it is an exciting car indeed. Italian influence pervaded the design of the M-1; in fact, Lamborghini originally began work on the car, but passed it on to BMW when development money ran out. Giorgetto Giugiaro, responsible for many of the wedge-shaped designs of the time, did the body. The mid-mounted engine, a 3.5-liter six, same as that used in the luxury BMW 635 CSi, put out 277 hp for road use but was boosted to as much as 850 for racing. Even the "tame" versions of the car would top 160 mph.

The M-1 premiered at the 1978 Paris Salon. Production totaled only about 450 cars, phasing out in mid-1981. BMW's conservative yet precisely built and very roadworthy cars, such as their 3-series and 6-series machines, had, since the early seventies, increasingly become the emblem of the young urban professional or "yuppie." While a spectacular machine, the maverick M-1 never really found a place in BMW's stable.

1980-1989

In a decade of ego and excess, men like John DeLorean make their dreams real. We are all encouraged to live our fantasies: Buy that Rolls or Lamborghini. . . Go for the checkered flag. . . Build that outrageous hot rod. . . Turn the family car into a dragster or a palace on wheels.

1981
DeLorean DMC-12 Sports Coupe

DeLoreans were special cars, but this one is unique, because it was signed by its creator, John Z. DeLorean, on the driver's side door jamb. DeLorean himself was nothing if not unique, attempting something that not even the legendary Preston Tucker could do: sell a mass-produced automobile in the teeth of competition from Detroit's Big Three. DeLorean left a high-flying 17-year career with General Motors to follow his dream.

He almost pulled it off. Stunning design studies by Ital Design's Giugiaro were unveiled in 1975, revealing a rear-engined fastback shaped like a tapered wedge, with angular body panels clad in stainless steel. By that time, millions in start-up capital were flowing in. But when, after agonizing delays, production finally started in Ireland in 1980, the styling was looking less fresh, despite the car's spectacular gullwing doors. The Renault-derived V-6 engine's performance proved disappointing, as did sales, even with dramatic price cuts. Insurmountable financial and legal problems plagued DeLorean; production halted in 1982 with only 7400 cars completed.

1982 Porsche 956

Racing's new "C" class category this year allowed creation of one of Porsche's and the world's most successful competition cars. The C Class covered closed GT prototype cars and enforced strict fuel-consumption limits. Though Porsche's 600-hp, turbo-charged, flat-six, 2.6-liter engine guzzled gas, compulsive attention to streamlining made the most of every gallon. Stretching the rules governing use of "ground effect"—note the zero ground clearance—helped glue the car to the road.

Derived from the model 936 open car, the 956 featured Porsche's first monocoque body using Kevlar composites. It weighed only 1900 pounds. A similar model 962 appeared later for American IMSA racing. The Number 001 prototype car is shown here at the Vuitton Concours. Carrying Rothmans colors, the now privately owned car won the 956's first race at Silverstone in 1982, and later that year it triumphed in Le Mans. Drivers were Jackie Ickx and Derek Bell. Many more victories followed, leading to an unprecedented string of seven Le Mans wins by Porsche.

1
BOSCH
BILSTEIN
DUNLOP
DUNLOP

1983 Rolls-Royce Corniche Convertible

It was, after all, the "Me Decade," and if you were one of Tom Wolfe's "Masters of the Universe" and desiring of a higher profile than afforded by the ho-hum Rolls-Royce Silver Spirit, you could opt for the Rolls Corniche convertible—perhaps in gold? Of course the "Spirit of Ecstasy" hood sculpture still faced proudly into the wind above that unchanging classic grille, providing unparalleled recognition value.

The Corniche two-door coupe was gone, but the convertible continued much the same as when introduced in 1971 by a Rolls-Royce recovering from bankruptcy. They proved exceedingly popular. The 412-cubic-inch V-8 gave "adequate" horsepower to push the 5000-pound car to 120 mph. Better breathing exhausts produced this respectable speed but gave the Corniche a low-pitched growl unsuitable for the standard Rolls-Royce. Bodies were by coachbuilder Mulliner-Park Ward and took almost half a year to complete. Dare we mention cost? A bit north of $160,000 in 1983 dollars.

1984 Lamborghini Countach 5000S

Another high-profile car, but this one with a real "bad boy" image. The Countach would have been the wheels of choice for a drug kingpin on the new hit TV show "Miami Vice." Even the Italian slang-derived name is a tad nasty.

Taking the multifaceted wedge-shaped look to the limits, and beyond, of an Earth-based vehicle, the Countach was first seen as an electrifying show car in 1971 and was sold in Europe starting in 1974. Its outrageous styling by Bertone's Marcello Gandini included semi-gullwing doors, a mid-engine layout, and an aluminum-skinned space-frame body. Countach's aggressive looks were backed up by superb road holding and near 200-mph speeds. By 1984, when this 5000S rolled out with a larger 4.7-liter V-12, U.S. environmental restrictions brought horsepower down to 325. A newer version was on its way, however—the 48-valve Quatrovalvole with 420 hp, available until 1989, when the new Diablo took up the flag for Lamborghini.

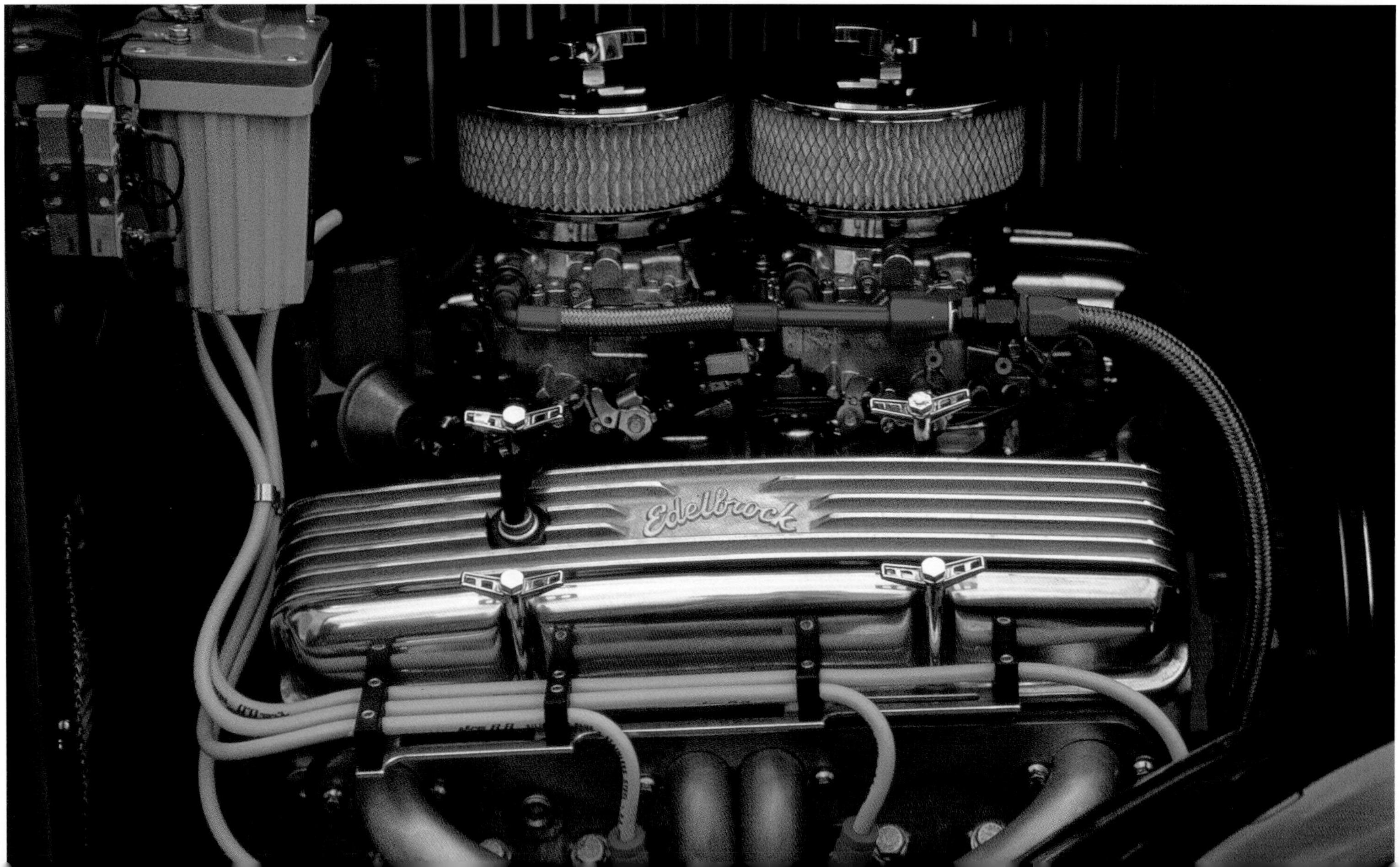
Edelbrock

1985
1926 Willys Hot Rod

By 1985, nostalgia for the hot rods of the fifties had the MTV generation burning rubber and cruisin' again, spurred on by the likes of the rock band ZZ Top's "Eliminator Coupe" in countless music videos. One result was this tasteful, almost stock-bodied 1926 Willys Overland Coupe, completed at the end of 1984. A formal-bodied Willys sedan may seem an odd choice for a custom rod, but the preferred alternatives, the perennial Deuce Coupe or 1932 Ford, were hard to come by then. Later Willys bodies are often seen as customs or rods, and those small-displacement Willys 77s of the thirties held their own in races with exotic European sports cars.

The fat, chrome wire wheels and lowered frame hint of what's under the hood. Starting with a Chevy 350 block, owner Neil MacMahon added Edelbrock cams and heads and Sanderson headers, topped off by two four-barreled carbs, bringing the horsepower to 450. Underneath, everything, including the stainless-steel floor pan, is chromed and polished. The interior looks almost original except for the front bucket seats.

1986 Ford RS 200

From the esoteric world of European rally competition comes a tiny bombshell from Ford in the U.K. The company decided in 1983 to go all out for the high-performance Class B rally title. Using interior elements from the Ford Sierra and a turbocharged Escort engine as starting points, Ford Motorsport engineers worked their magic. A roof-mounted ram-air scoop fed the little rear-mounted 1800-cc engine, which now pushed 250 hp (up to 450 in some models) through a front-mounted, five-speed transaxle driving all four wheels. The Kevlar body shell was by Bertone of Italy.

The car's rookie season brought spectacular wins—four major rally championships and 21 victories overall, but this brief taste of glory was all that was to be allowed to the RS 200. The B Class was eliminated the next year—too dangerous, said racing officials. Ford had produced 200 of the cars and claimed they were docile enough for street use, but Kurt Porucks, owner of this stubby "Super Bee," says, "No way!"

1987 Buick Regal Grand National

The mid-eighties saw the reappearance in the Buick line-up of what could only be called (gasp!) performance cars. Buick, the family car personified, again had some models worthy of comparison to its muscle-car-era GSX. Since 1978 Buick had offered turbocharged, or "T Series," engines, but in 1984 they produced the Grand National option package, with a turbocharged, intercooled, and fuel-injected 3.8-liter V-6.

Look at Allan La Foe of New Jersey's award-winning 1987 Grand National in all its sinister glory. Everything, it seems, that can be black is black: air dam, spoiler, bumpers, and headlight bezels. The only hint of what is under that hood is the fuel-pressure gauge Velcroed to the windshield. The car's already potent V-6 has a bigger turbo and bigger injectors installed and now produces upwards of 480 hp. Its official time through the quarter-mile is 11.77 seconds and 114 mph. The 1987s were the last rear-wheel-drive turbos made by Buick and proved so popular that production lines stayed open until December, long after the switch to 1988 models was due.

1988 Lincoln Mark VII Bill Blass Edition

The first Mark VII appeared in 1984, and along with the previous year's Thunderbird, became the first of a radical new breed from Ford that eventually influenced all the world's automobiles. Gone were the flat-sided boxes of the seventies. The new look was rounded and aerodynamic, and the design tool of choice was the wind tunnel.

By 1988, the whole Ford line-up, including the futuristic new Taurus and Sable, had received the "aero" treatment, but the Mark VII was holding up well, and only minor changes were made. Bill Blass and Gianni Versace were apparently asked for their thoughts on the cars. Mr. Blass's contributions, seen here, consisted of paint trim and striping, wire spoke wheels, and leather or Ultrasuede upholstery. The car shown is stock except for blacked-out windows and headlights and a killer sound system. Also available was a performance-package LSC model. Every conceivable convenience seemed to be standard equipment on these cars.

Radial T/A

1989 1926 Model T Hot Rod

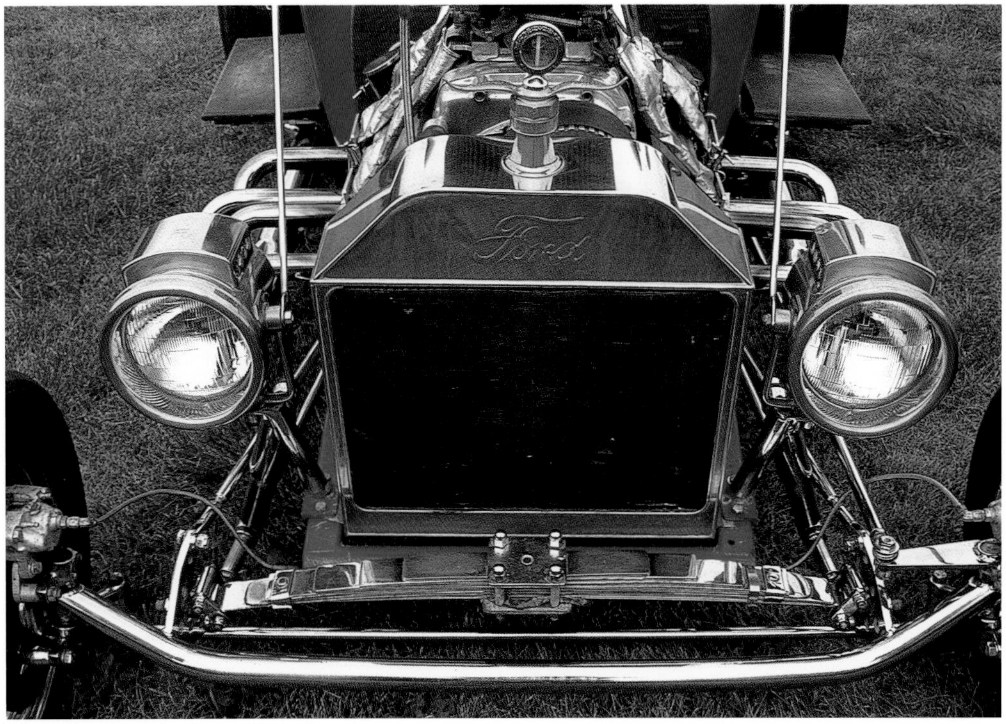

Fascination with the fifties' hot-rod culture by everyone from the "Boomers" on down showed no sign of abating as the eighties ended. Every aspect of the old "Kalifornia Kar Kulture" was re-explored—rods, customs, dragsters, funny-cars—and new hybrids bloomed, like monster trucks and the bouncing cars called "low-riders" by their Latino creators.

This circa-1989 machine is a fantasy on the Model T, the one that started it all, whose little four-cylinder engine cried out to be hotted up and whose already lightweight body could be stripped further for more speed. Later the model A and the 1932 Ford would displace the "T," but this particular "homage to Henry" takes us back to show cars of the early sixties by such greats as Dean Jeffries and "Big Daddy" Roth. Keeping little more than the roadster "bucket-T" body and the headstone radiator, an oversize padded top with "cathedral windows" is added, making for a true show car. The "go" is there as well: witness the monster blower that completely engulfs the engine and the chrome lakes pipes. Antique brass headlights and tail lights keep things from getting too serious, however.

1990
Mazda MX-5 Miata Roadster

Here's a Miata with an attitude. Not content with the cute, simple, little Mazda that made owning a sports car affordable again, owner Orlando Trancho has turned his 1990 MX-5 into one fire-breathing machine. Most obvious is a "Type V Combat Kit" that adds air dam, side skirts, and spoiler. Wheels now have 17-inch racing rims. The interior is from a 1994 "M-Edition" Miata, with leather and wood trim and a custom surround-sound system. Under the hood is a turbocharger with intercooler that helps get quarter-mile times down to 14.6 seconds. Just visible is a subtle, airbrushed checker flag that graces the left front fender.

Most Miata owners love their cars just as they are, however. The original design plays off of British sports cars of the fifties, and the sixties-era Lotus Élan in particular. When introduced in 1989 a feeding frenzy ensued, driving prices way over the $14,000 list. Demand still seems healthy, and for 1998, a major restyling got a warm reception.

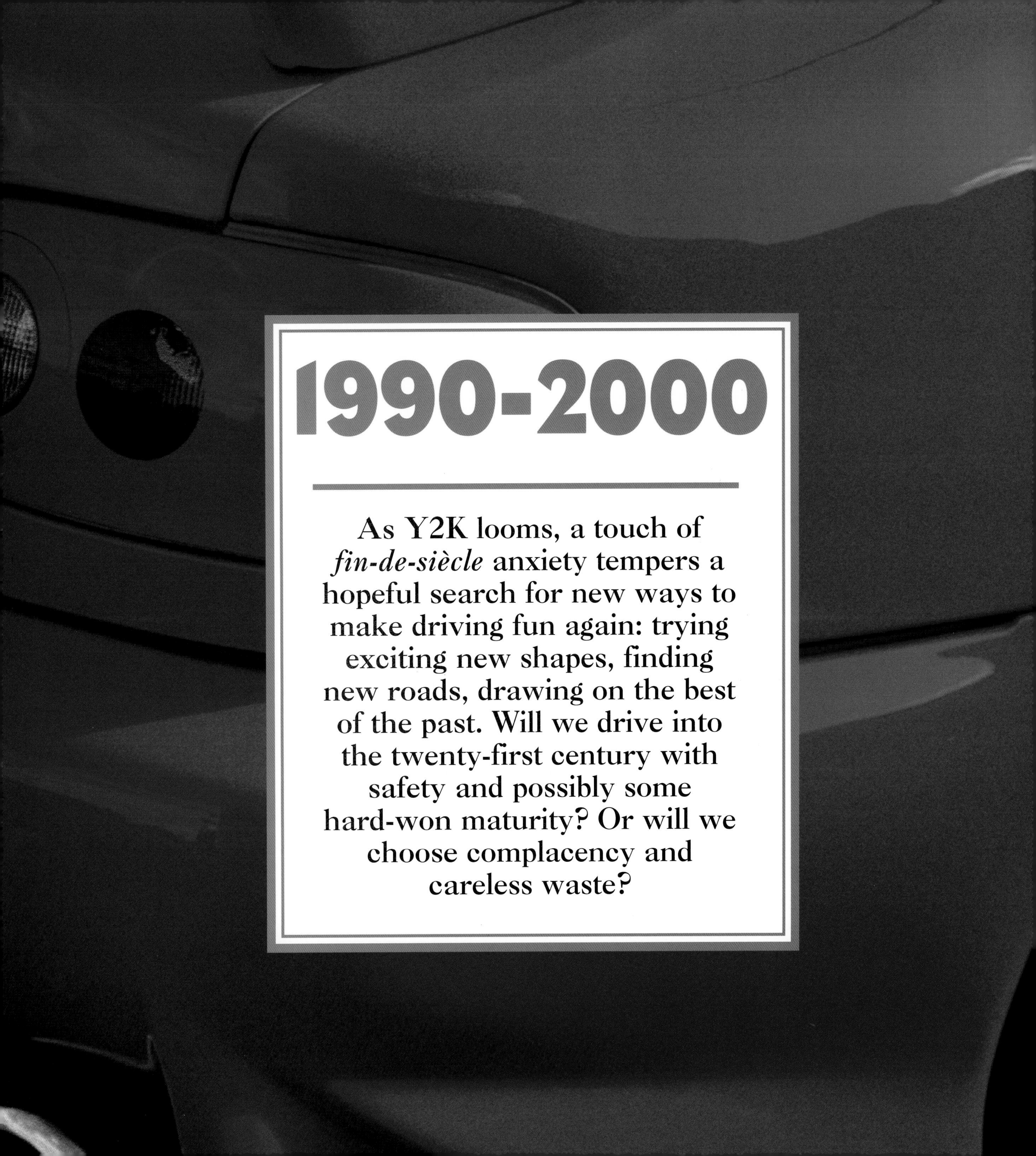

1990-2000

As Y2K looms, a touch of *fin-de-siècle* anxiety tempers a hopeful search for new ways to make driving fun again: trying exciting new shapes, finding new roads, drawing on the best of the past. Will we drive into the twenty-first century with safety and possibly some hard-won maturity? Or will we choose complacency and careless waste?

1991 Chevrolet Corvette Convertible

It is every kid's fantasy car, the embodiment of America's wanderlust and need for speed. It is the Corvette, star of song and story, movie and TV show—"Corvette Summer" and "Route 66" come to mind—that celebrate fast traveling for its own sake.

From its birth in 1953 as a sporty little puppy of a car that GM styling director Harley Earl thought his son might take to college, through the potent and sharklike 1963 Sting Ray, created as the personal car of Earl's successor Bill Mitchell, right up until the present day, the 'Vette has remained America's only true production sports car.

Kicking off the 1990s with the restyling of a body that had been virtually unchanged since introduced in 1984, the 1991 Corvette now had the square tail lights previously worn only by the high-powered ZR-1 models. This one, shown in Steel Blue, has the stock 5.7-liter, 350-cubic-inch L98 engine. An all-new, much heralded "Fifth Series" Corvette did not arrive until 1997.

1992 Chrysler LeBaron Convertible

Looking unfashionably retro amongst the slippery shapes of the nineties is this slab-sided, but trim, ragtop. It is one of the last of the "K-Cars," a Chrysler LeBaron convertible, marking its tenth anniversary this year. But give the car its due. Not only did the K-platform all but save the Chrysler Corporation, but it reintroduced the full-size (well, almost full-size) convertible and the joys of top-down driving to the beleaguered U.S. public. Thirteen thousand Americans anted up almost $14,000 for the privilege that first year. In subsequent years, one could even relive the forties' glory of the wood-bedecked Town and Country Chryslers.

In 1987, LeBaron went under the knife and emerged with some shapelier curves and even hidden headlights, looking much like this 1992 model. By then, besides the standard four and turbocharged four, a Mitsubishi-built V-6 was available as well as four-wheel disk brakes and ABS. By 1994 and 1995, only the convertible LeBaron was offered, and in 1996 came the gorgeous, roomy Sebring, worlds ahead of the old K-box.

1993 Cadillac Eldorado Sport Coupe

In the forty years since the first Eldorado Convertible in 1953, Cadillac had used the evocative mythic name for cars that were a cut above the standard. That first Eldorado, of which only 500 were made, introduced the "panoramic" windshield. Others, such as the 1957 Eldorado Brougham and the 1976 Eldo convertible, built on the legend. But in the mid-eighties there had been little to choose between Eldorado and the Seville, formerly a four-door-only model.

The new 1992 model, though, seemed to have pegged the market squarely. Still sharing a basic platform with Seville, but targeted at a more conservative client than the Seville's more Eurocentric driver, Eldorado became an elegant, sure-footed touring coupe. New for 1993 was the Northstar engine, rated at 270 hp in the Sport Coupe and 295 hp in the Touring Coupe. Computers, of course, proliferated. The transmission now sensed your driving style, and Ride-Sensing Suspension adjusted handling to match road conditions.

Though derided in 1986 as a "jelly bean," the Taurus was actually a poker chip with which Ford gambled its corporate future. Market share was eroding and losses snowballing in 1980 when development started. Management would try something totally, desperately new. Typical was the body design by Jack Telnack

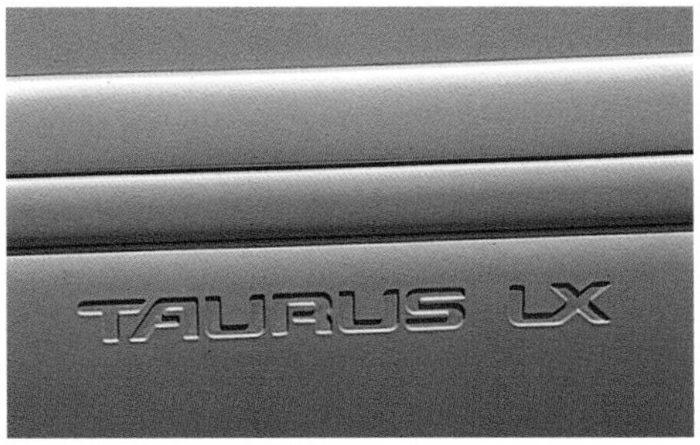

with a drag ratio of 0.33. Aerodynamic efficiency would help burn less fuel, projected to be scarce and expensive in the 1990s. Under the skin, more innovation—more comfortable seating, logical controls, new engines and powertrains. After some early problems, the Taurus settled in, becoming a "cash bull" for Ford, though Honda gradually edged into a commanding lead in sales.

1994 Ford Taurus LX Sedan

The Taurus first appeared in 1986, but by 1994 it no longer looked as outrageous as it had back then. The car's looks were still unique enough to make a believable "police car of the future" in the 1990 movie "Robocop," but Ford actually backtracked with some design elements. In 1992 and again in 1995 they moved away from the original blacked-out, one-piece look of the window glass to more visible, and more conventional, painted rear-door pillars.

1995 Buick Riviera Coupe

One sign of the resurgence of a distinctly American direction in car design was Buick's new Riviera Coupe. With a rich heritage dating back to the original 1963 Riviera, Bill Mitchell's classic brainchild, the new machine had a lot to live up to. In terms of style, the 1995 Riv redefined the breed. Riviera uses the same 114-inch-wheelbase platform as Oldsmobile's Aurora, whose lean and hungry-looking body shares no sheet metal with the curvaceous Buick. Styled by GM veteran Bill Porter, the car has its roots in Buick's 1991 Lucerne concept car, with lines that Porter calls "both muscular and romantic," with "a hint of mystery." Drivetrain components differ from Aurora also: at first, a 3.8-liter V-6 with or without supercharger was available, but later models came only with "blowers." Interior fittings were styled by Paul Tatseos, though the look was almost too austere.

These large coupes, while critically acclaimed, have not sold well, and 1999 marked Riviera's last year—in this century—except for a limited edition of 200 "Silver Arrow" models with special paint schemes.

1996 Chrysler Atlantic Concept Car

Lately, Chrysler has been mining the gold of classic automobile shapes of the past with its successful Heritage Design program. Chrysler's top designer, Tom Gale, hopes to revitalize car design by imbuing his company's machines with the spirit and style of past eras, updated for today. First came the sixties' racing Cobra-inspired Dodge Viper, then the Plymouth Prowler, seen later in this book. In 1996, Chrysler contemplated reentering the luxury car market, and show cars like the Atlantic and the later Chronos show the direction of Chrysler's thinking.

Named for the celebrated Bugatti 57S Atlantic, Chrysler's grandly proportioned coupe recalls many design cues from that thirties' masterwork, most prominently the crease or peak running from hood through roof to tail of the car. The engine is a one of a kind straight eight, also a la Bugatti, but Chrysler designers claim additional inspiration from French custom coachbuilders of the late thirties. Wheels are larger than life—21 inches in front and 22 inches in the rear—surely worthy of tracking the wheel prints of these greats. Rumors are that 100 Atlantics were to have been built. Let's hope their owners get them out onto the road where they can be seen.

1997 Honda CR-V

It is not really a car, though it sits on a Honda Civic chassis; it is not a truck, since it holds only half as much as a minivan. It is a "Comfortable Runabout Vehicle," and it seems to be just what the driving public wants. American roads are filling with Sport Utility Vehicles, with sizes ranging from small through titanic. By 1998, Honda was selling 100,000 CR-Vs a year. What's not to like about these mini-SUVs? They're high-sitting, four-wheel-drive station wagons that get better mileage than full-size Sport-Utes and handle much like cars. And the price for this 1997 model came to around $20,000. Power at first was meager but has since climbed to 145 hp. Engaging the four-wheel drive is a nonevent; the rear wheels engage automatically with any loss of front-wheel traction. But though road clearance is high, this "Runabout Vehicle" is not a serious off-road machine. The interior is quite flexible for all kinds of haulage, and a nifty extra is a foldout picnic table!

HONDA

1998 Plymouth Prowler

The Prowler started as a suggestion on a 3 x 5 card for a "hot-rod-style retro car." If that proposal sounds unlikely for a Big Three automaker to not only build but place into production, you haven't been watching Chrysler recently. Chrysler's then-President Bob Lutz and design chief Tom Gale, both true "car guys," got the idea moving in 1990, and by 1993

the concept car blew people away at the Detroit Auto Show. So positive was the reception that production plans began almost immediately. The Prowler premiered in 1997.

The final car partakes more of the flashy hand-built rods of the seventies typified by the work of Boyd Coddington, while retaining little more than the tail-up, shovel-nose stance of the fifties' "highboy" rods. All the gear is nineties' state of the art, from aluminum body and frame to 3.5-liter, overhead-cam V-6 and four-speed, automatic-stick transmission. For 1998 the "yard-deep" purple finish is joined by bright yellow, doubling the choice of colors.

1999 Volvo S80 Sedan

Shifting attention now to issues beyond the selfish pleasures of driving, to look at an automaker traditionally concerned with matters of safety and social responsibility, sure to be a prime focus in the next century. To those who are not "car people," the automobile is little more than a rolling appliance. It must be reliable, dependable, comfortable, quiet, and above all safe. This is Volvo's special niche.

The all-new flagship Volvo S80, as always, leads in new safety features, like whiplash protection, "Inflatable Curtains" for side-impact crashes, two types of stability controls, and a Brake Force Distribution system to shorten stopping distances. Performance is not neglected: the S80 competes with BMW, Lexus, and Mercedes, so an optional turbocharged six gives 268 hp and 0-60 times of 6.5 seconds. Though the styling is less than earthshaking, it is pleasant and contemporary, with a signature lowered belt line that runs right through the tail lights. A low aerodynamic drag rating of 0.28 assures Volvo drivers of a swift, safe passage into the new millennium.

2000 Audi TT Sport Coupe

But then again, a good part of driving is about fun. At the turn of the last century, motoring was a sport and a recreation. With the coming of cars like the Miata, the BMW Z-car, and the Porsche Boxster in the 1990s, something of that spirit has returned, and the Audi TT raises the excitement level a notch for 2000.

Driving in 1900 was also about the love of mechanism for its own sake. Gleaming cylinders and gears, machined surfaces, the noise of power. This and the legacy of the German Bauhaus industrial design movement of the 1930s, which emphasized clean, geometric forms, shows in the styling of the TT. Its design uses the circle as a major design motif—only fitting in an Audi whose logo features four interlocked circles.

Our photo gives just a titillating glimpse of what will grow into a whole family of TTs as the new century begins: a roadster, four-wheel-drive Quattro models, and a high-performance 225-hp machine.

The Automobile in the Next Century

Prophets have been predicting the demise of the auto in the twenty-first-century world of the future since the twentieth began. At first, it was felt the "fad" would die out. Then prognosticators saw replacements in the newer technologies of the moment. Airplanes would become "aerial run-abouts," or autogiros would give us freedom from earthbound roads. After World War II, there would be an airplane in every garage. Inventions such as monorails, zeppelins, and people-moving beltways would make the car obsolete. Uncontrollable traffic jams and gasoline shortages would force the revitalization of public transport. At the very least, new methods of propulsion would dominate. Electric motors, beamed microwaves, turbine engines, and even atomic powerplants must surely supplant the noisy, polluting, and inefficient internal-combustion engine.

But the humble gasoline-powered auto will be with us for as far into the twenty-first century as we can foresee. Other propulsion technologies will, so far, play a supplementary role, from electrics, to fuel cells, to so-called "hybrid" mixes. There is really no way to predict which of them may make commercial sense, so here are some snapshots of actual machines from various manufacturers' idea factories.

The Dodge ESX-2 concept car *(right)* from Daimler Chrysler, is a Mybrid or "mild hybrid" using a diesel for primary power and electricity for high-demand acceleration only. Other advanced features are an aluminum frame, aerodynamic molded plastic body, and low-loss transmission, all combining to give 70 mpg, low emissions, and lively performance.

Ford takes another approach. Although it is working on the hydrogen-fuel-cell-powered P-2000 sedan and other hybrid technologies, it has invested in a Norwegian company that produces a lightweight plastic-bodied electric city car, the cute-as-a-bug Th!nk *(lower left)*, already on sale in Europe.

We've seen how some companies, notably Chrysler, look to the past for ways to foster new takes on old ideas with unabashedly retro styling. An example of this approach is the thirties' proportioned Chrysler PT Cruiser *(upper right)*. An early version, the Pronto Cruizer, is shown here. Designed by Bryan Nesbitt, it is called a "segment buster," as it combines hatchback, station wagon, and SUV elements within its hot-rod-inspired exterior. Love it or hate it, this high-roofed look is certain to be emulated.

Another segment-busting category might be the ultra-high-priced vehicle. First to go on sale is the Mercedes Maybach *(middle right)*. With the economy in high gear, some automakers feel there is a market for these rolling palaces. VW has plans for a $600,000, 18-cylinder-powered revival of the Bugatti. The $350,000 Maybach flaunts translucent graphite composite fenders and a pull-down HDTV screen in its wood-and-silver-trimmed rear compartment. Shades of the Roaring Twenties!

Finally, though the SUV phenomenon is really beyond this book's scope, we can't resist Chrysler's ultimate take on the "mine is bigger than yours" luxury truck: The Dodge Power Wagon concept vehicle *(bottom)*. It is humongous, high tech, and supposedly environmentally friendly, since it burns sulfur-free "designer fuels."

So the gasoline-powered automobile is not out of the race yet, and here you have seen some of the industry's best answers to the question: What kinds of "horseless carriages" will take us down that twenty-first-century highway?

Automobile Museums and Automobile Web Sites

We thank the many dedicated individuals at these fantastic institutions who have assisted us over the years. Of course there are many other fine collections, too numerous to list, that are also worth a visit. Please note that many of the Web addresses listed here are commercial sites. This should not be construed as a recommendation by either the authors or the publishers for any of the products or services listed at these sites.

Alamo Classic Car Showcase & Museum
6401 S Interstate 35
New Braunfels, TX 78132
(210)606-4311; fax (210)620-4387

Auburn Cord Duesenberg Museum
1600 South Wayne Street
P.O. Box 271
Auburn, IN 46706
(219)925-1444
http://www.classicar.com/museums/auburn

National Motor Museum at Beaulieu
John Montagu Building
Beaulieu, Brockenhurst
Hampshire, SO42 7ZN
England
0590-612345; fax 0590-612655
http://www.beaulieu.co.uk/museum/index.html

The Blackhawk Auto Museum
1092 Eagles Nest Place
Danville, CA 94506
(510)736-0695; fax (510)736-7479

Harrah National Automobile Museum
10 Lake Street South
Reno, NV 89501
(702)333-9300; fax (702)333-9309

Henry Ford Museum & Greenfield Village
20900 Oakwood Boulevard
Dearborn, MI 48120
(313)271-1620
http://www.hfmgv.org/

The Museum of Transportation
Larz Anderson Park
15 Newton Street
Brookline, MA 02146
(617)522-6547
http://www.mot.org/

Old Rhinebeck Aerodrome
44 Stone Church Road
Rhinebeck, NY 12572
(914)758-8610
http://www.oldrhinebeck.org/

Owls Head Transportation Museum
P.O. Box 277
Owls Head, ME 04854
(207)594-4418
http://www.ohtm.org/

Petersen Automotive Museum
6060 Wilshire Boulevard
Los Angeles, CA 90036
(213)930-CARS

Studebaker
Studebaker National Museum, Inc.
525 South Main Street
South Bend, IN 46601
(219)235-9714

Organizations and Associations

Almost every organization of this type has a Web site. If you are not online, you can access these sites at your local library. There you will find listings of literally thousands of clubs and organizations that cater to every specialty. Just a sampling of some of the better known are listed here.

Antique Automobile Club of America
AACA National Headquarters
501 W. Governor Road
P.O. Box 417
Hershey, PA 17033
(717)534-1910
http://www.aaca.org/

Classic Car Club of America
http://www.classiccarclub.org

Classic cars in general
http://www.classiccar.com

Car Club and Other Listings

These two Web sites give extensive listings for all types of car clubs worldwide, from customs, dragsters, and hot rods, to classics, fifties cruisers, and low riders:
http://carclubs.com/carclubs.htm
http://www.carlist.com/carclub.html

Horseless Carriage Club of America
http://www.horseless.com

Hot Rods
http://www.rodder.com

Vintage Auto Racing Assoc. (VARA)
http://www.vararacing.com/

Watkins Glen (historic racing)
http://www.theglen.com

Manufacturers' Web Sites

For existing marques of autos, only the Web sites of the major manufacturers are listed here. The individual brands within the parent companies are accessible from these sites. For historical marques we list a selection of enthusiast-run sites or museums. Almost every marque that has ever existed has a club and/or Web site.

Only a selection from the cars covered in the book can be shown here.

Auburn, Cord, and Duesenberg
See museum listing.

Audi
http://www.audi.com/

BMW
http://www.bmw.com/bmwe/homepage/index.html

Bugatti
http://www.stud.ntnu.no/~jacob/BILsidor/Bugatti/info/Links.html

Daimler Chrysler
http://www.daimlerchrysler.com/products/products_e/index_e.html

DeLorean
http://www.valzog.com/delorean/

Ford
http://www2.ford.com/default.asp

GM
http://www.gm.com/

Honda
http://www.honda1999.com/

Jeep
http://www.jeepunpaved.com/frameset_home.html

Jaguar
http://www.jaguar.com/

Lamborghini
http://lamborghini.itg.net/

Mazda Miata
http://www.miata.net/mca/
or
http://www.mazdausa.com/home.asp

Packard
http://www.packardclub.org/

Porsche
http://www.porsche.com/

Rolls-Royce and Bentley
http://www.rolls-royceandbentley.co.uk/company.html

Rolls historic (Rolls-Royce owners club)
http://www.rroc.org/

Toyota Land Cruiser
http://www.vtr.org/

Triumph
http://www.vtr.org/

Volkswagen
http://www3.vw.com/index4.html

Volvo
http://www.volvocars.com/home/index.html

Photo Credits

Except for the following list, all photographs copyright 1999 by Fredric Winkowski and Frank D. Sullivan.

Page 36 (1918): Photo courtesy the National Motor Museum, Beaulieu, Hampshire, U.K.

Page 40 (1921): Photo by N. Wright/ National Motor Museum, Beaulieu, Hampshire, U.K.

Page 44 (1925): Photos by John Tankrd, courtesy of Conrad Schaub

Page 55 (1932): Photo by John Tankrd, courtesy of Conrad Schaub

Page 124 (1972): Photos by Conrad Schaub

Pages 162-163: Dodge ESX-2, Future Pronto Cruizer AWD, Mercedes-Benz Maybach, Dodge Power Wagon Concept Vehicle, photos all copyright Daimler Chrysler, used by permission.

Page 162: Future Ford Th!nk Electric City Car, photo copyright Ford Motor Company, used by permission.

Acknowledgments and Thanks

This is the place to thank the owners of the pictured machines, who devote so much time to their upkeep and restoration, and especially those who graciously invited us into their homes and garages with our cameras, patiently telling us about their car's unique history.

Jonathan Day, Tom Wood, and Elly at the National Motor Museum, Beaulieu; George and Manny Dragone at Dragone Classic Motors in Bridgeport, CT; Chuck Spielman at Only Yesterday Classic Autos in Port Washington, NY; the staff at the SIBL Library in New York City; Bill Keating and Son at Keating Motors in Hamden, CT; Kurt Poruks and crew at Ridgewood Motor Classics in Ridgewood, NJ; Chris Heady, John Inuson, and Howie Prager at the New Hackensack Fire Company in Wappingers Falls, NY; Mike Geylin, Fred Heiler, and John Herlitz at Daimler Chrysler; Kathleen Hamilton at Ford; Galen Fike, Jim Hare, Ken Kassen, Gene LaMarco, and Bob McKenzie at Old Rhinebeck Aerodrome; Rick Fox, John Lothrop, Robin Maddalena, Dave Manzi, Dawn Meldrum, George Roberts, and Dick Sedgewick at Brookline; Nadine Johnson & Associates and all the other helpful people at the Vuitton Concours in New York; the staff at the Greenwich Concours in Connecticut; the staff at the Lehigh Concours in Pennsylvania; and special thanks to Marilyn Bliss, Muriel Mentze, Jon Lopez, Frank Skorski, Conrad Schaub, and Floyd Paycheck.

We extend our deepest gratitude to: Nick Allegretta, Bob Blanck, Ruth Bonomo, David Campbell, Judge Joseph C. Cassini III, John Tom Cohoe, Lee Davenport, Reid Echandia, Donald Eckel, Charles Eggert, Walter and Naiad Einsel, Douglas Fernandez, Bill Fetzke and Bill Fetzke Jr., Yaron Fiddler, Thomas Fleming, Ken Ganz, Michael Germane, Walter Helstowski, John Henry, Jay Hirsch, Van Horneff, John H. Hovey, Joseph and Cathy Janichko, Robert Kane Jr., Charles Kern, Beverly Rae Kimes, Don Klotz, Don Koleman, Alan LaFoe, Curt Lawson, Nick Lusito, Neil MacMahon, Ed Moreno, Stephanie O'Keeffe, Mark Pelham, Dr. Marcel and Renee Perlman, Tom Portesi, Reed Rickman, Robert Rooke, Alan Rubinstein, Charles Runyan, Manfred Ryan, Joe Sagarese, Bob Sage, Klaus Saurbier, Charles and Kathy Scott, Jim Simpson, Herb Singe, Edward Spannhake, Leslie Spurlock, Bill Stevens, John Tankrd, Mike Toomey, Orlando Trancho, Mr. and Mrs. Thomas Troxell, Dennis Wilsea, Paul Wilson, Frank Zabski Jr., Diane Zapach, and all the many other enthusiasts who shared their time and expertise with us and made this project such a joyful and rewarding experience.

INDEX